# 100 DAYS TO
# FREEDOM

from

## Fear and Anxiety

## Daily Devotional

STEPHEN ARTERBURN

AspirePress

# 100 Days to Freedom
## from Fear and Anxiety

Copyright © 2021 Stephen Arterburn
All rights reserved.
Published by Aspire Press
An imprint of Hendrickson Publishing Group
Rose Publishing, LLC
P.O. Box 3473
Peabody, Massachusetts 01961-3473 USA
www.HendricksonPublishingGroup.com

ISBN: 9781628629965

Written with Becky L. Brown

Book cover and layout design by Sergio Urquiza

Printed by APS

February 2021, 1st Printing

This book is given to

_____

on this day

_____

# Contents

# Introduction

Do you have a fearful heart? An anxious feeling that things are out of control and you cannot imagine it getting any better? Even as Christ-followers who believe what the Word of God says, we can experience fear and anxiety. Does that mean we really don't believe? Or that we are not living "right"? Some of us have heard from well-meaning people that we just don't need to worry—God's got it all under control!

Fear and anxiety can control our lives, so let's spend the next 100 days finding freedom from the anxiety and fear that overwhelm us and keep us from experiencing the peace of Christ. The scriptures you will read—the devotionals, quotes, and prayers—will begin to change the way you think and feel. While your circumstances may be challenging, you can find peace in the storms of life!

# Freedom!

*I am leaving you with a gift—peace of mind and heart.*
*And the peace I give is a gift the world cannot give.*
*So don't be troubled or afraid.*

JOHN 14:27

An anxious mind and a fearful heart can create a spin cycle that interrupts your normal thought process. You feel caught in a centrifuge, and momentum keeps you stuck thinking about all the many reasons you are anxious and fearful. Panic sets in and feels dizzying and overwhelming!

If you have been in this cycle, you know how challenging it can be to get out of the spin—challenging, but not impossible. When it happens, the most important—and the most difficult—step to take is to *stop*. Take a breath and refocus. Remind yourself that God has a plan for you and that it is good. Let this truth soak in and help.

If possible, connect with someone you trust and talk through the issue until you have stopped spinning. Then create a plan for when and if it happens again. A simple phrase like "God's got this" or "Lord, bring me peace" can interrupt the cycle and exert a powerful influence on thinking and emotions. You were created by God and God will see you through!

The little troubles and worries of life may be as stumbling blocks in our way, or we may make them stepping-stones to a nobler character and to Heaven. Troubles are often the tools by which God fashions us for better things.

Henry Ward Beecher

Our lives are full of "supposes." Suppose this should happen, or suppose that should happen; what could we do; how could we bear it? But, if we are dwelling in the high tower of the dwelling place of God, all these supposes will drop out of our lives. We shall be "quiet from the fear of evil," for no threatenings of evil can penetrate into the high tower of God.

Hannah Whitall Smith

## For further reflection

Joshua 1:6-9; 1 Timothy 6:11-12;
2 Thessalonians 2:16-17

## TODAY'S PRAYER

Lord Jesus, you know my heart, my fear and my anxiety. Help me to begin to trust you with the things that cause me to worry and fret. Lord, I need your strength and peace as I go throughout my day. I pray you would bless me with your presence. And that your glory would be revealed in me. Amen.

# Day 2

## Strong and Encouraged

*Don't be afraid, for I am with you.*
*Don't be discouraged, for I am your God.*
*I will strengthen you and help you. I will*
*hold you up with my victorious right hand.*

ISAIAH 41:10

When fear and anxiety have been ruling our days, it can be so irritating to have someone say, "Don't worry!" or "Cheer up!" They may mean well, or they may feel ill-equipped to help you. But if it were that easy to just not feel the way we are feeling, we wouldn't feel this way! No one wants to experience worry and uncertainty, yet it has become part of our daily journey.

What do you do when you recognize that worry has become your default? Or that your reactions are a bit over the edge? Many different types of anxiety can affect us—and it can be very important to seek help to understand the specific way it is affecting you. We might resist seeking help because, after all, that might cause anxiety, too! But beginning a plan to address what you are dealing with is so important to feeling better.

Perhaps you have the strength to reach out for help today. It might be just a phone call to a friend to say, "I think I need help for anxiety." Sharing these feelings with another for the first time may be the most difficult. When we feel

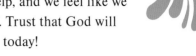

anxious, we think nothing will help, and we feel like we should know what to do for relief. Trust that God will provide help and strength for you today!

Worry is the antithesis of trust. You simply cannot do both. They are mutually exclusive.

Elisabeth Elliot

Worry does not empty tomorrow of its sorrow; it empties today of its strength.

Corrie ten Boom

On days when life is difficult and I feel overwhelmed, as I do fairly often, it helps to remember in my prayers that all God requires of me is to trust Him and be His friend. I find I can do that.

Bruce Larson

## For further reflection

2 Corinthians 12:8-10; Lamentations 3:21-25, 31-32

## TODAY'S PRAYER

Heavenly Father, give me the assurance of your strength and encourage me as I seek answers to the worries in my life. Help me to trust you with my needs. Amen.

# Day 3

## No Fear!

*I prayed to the Lord, and he answered me.*
*He freed me from all my fears.*

PSALM 34:4

Living in fear doesn't begin as a choice. No one decides to live their life afraid of everything. It develops as we experience things that are indeed scary and frightening. Fear also can be a result of living with people who have fears of their own—it can be contagious!

The strange thing about fear is that many times it cannot be identified. Rather, it is a feeling of uncertainty, dread, and the unknown. Our imagination can run wild with the endless possibilities of what could go wrong, dangers that lurk, and uncertainty about the future. Even if none of those may not have any basis in reality, "what if" may rule our thoughts.

Now, it can be helpful to have some concern about the unknown. Yet when we are overcome and obsessed with things that cannot be known, it traps us. Instead, recognize that life does present risks, you have survived a lot of them up to this point, and will face more in the future. When faced with fear, choose to unite your faith with your fear—be strengthened by the knowledge that while you may be afraid, you can trust that God will provide all you need to get you through the challenges of life!

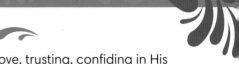

Living by faith in Jesus above, trusting, confiding in His great love; from all harm safe in His sheltering arm, I'm living by faith and feel no alarm.

James Wells

Beloved, I say, let your fears go, lest they make you fainthearted. Stop inspiring fear in those around you and now take your stand in faith. God has been good and He will continue to manifest His goodness. . . . Let us approach these days expecting to see the goodness of the Lord manifest. Let us be strong and of good courage, for the Lord will fight for us if we stand in faith.

Francis Frangipane

Anxiety and fear are like baby tigers: The more you feed them, the stronger they grow.

Billy Graham

## FOR FURTHER REFLECTION

Romans 8:35-39; Psalm 61:1-5; Ephesians 6:10-18

## TODAY'S PRAYER

Thank you, Lord, for your assurance when I am afraid. Provide your wisdom as I begin to identify the things that cause me to fear and to shrink back in my life. Help me to be bold in asking for help and give me courage for those things that need to be challenged. I ask this in the powerful name of Jesus. Amen.

# What If?

*Don't worry about anything; instead, pray about*
*everything. Tell God what you need, and thank him*
*for all he has done. Then you will experience God's*
*peace, which exceeds anything we can understand.*
*His peace will guard your hearts and minds*
*as you live in Christ Jesus.*

PHILIPPIANS 4:6-7

I t would be so helpful to know what is coming around the corner—like having one of those strange mirrors that lets you see from an angle, so you don't run into anything. With video recorders available to make sure everything is secure on our property—our front porch, the nursery—we have become accustomed to being alerted to the unexpected dangers that life may bring.

But what if you don't know everything? The truth is, you don't—and that is what causes so much worry. Although technology has given us the ability to know *some* of what we didn't know before, we simply cannot know everything. We desire to have control over our world, and when we cannot, anxiety creeps in. By worrying over things we cannot control, that anxiety thrives. Instead, recognizing your limitations of control and knowledge will begin to bring peace of mind.

Choose today to recognize your limitations. You wouldn't want to have total control if you knew what it would cost you. The anxiety that is controlling your life can be released as you turn over the things you cannot control to an Almighty God who is able—and is sovereign—and, most importantly, loves you!

Fear arises when we imagine everything depends on us.

Elisabeth Elliot

The more you pray, the less you'll panic. The more you worship, the less you worry. You'll feel more patient and less pressured.

Rick Warren

## FOR FURTHER REFLECTION

Matthew 7:7-8; 2 Corinthians 1:8-11;
Ephesians 1:18-21

## TODAY'S PRAYER

Lord Jesus, you know my urge to have it all under control. Help me in the unexpected to recognize you are Sovereign. Increase my peace in you and remind me of your love and care for me. In your name, Amen.

# Living Life

*And I am convinced that nothing can ever separate us from God's love. Neither death nor life, neither angels nor demons, neither our fears for today nor our worries about tomorrow—not even the powers of hell can separate us from God's love. No power in the sky above or in the earth below—indeed, nothing in all creation will ever be able to separate us from the love of God that is revealed in Christ Jesus our Lord.*

ROMANS 8:38-39

The fear of dying prevents so many people from really living. The fear that something will take your life can make you focus on the details of death, loss and suffering. You might be afraid of a loved one dying and how terrible the loss will be. Sometimes when fear wants to rule our lives it can cause us to stay in the alert mode even on the days where nothing much is happening. The difficulty about this kind of fear is that it is based partly in truth—we will all die at some point.

As difficult as this truth may be, acceptance will be the key to unlock this fear. When we avoid reality, we miss out on some of the true gifts of life. Challenging days can bring a richness to the days that are easier. We can begin to appreciate how precious each day is—even when they are boring!

Begin today to trust God with the beginning, middle and end of your life. Trust God with your loved one's lives. God loves us eternally. When we accept this truth, we can begin to live life fully—grateful for each day, and recognizing the gifts God presents to us, even amidst challenges. Make the most of what God has given you in your life for his glory, and experience life to the full—just as he had planned!

The best decisions aren't made when you're afraid of dying; the best decisions are made when you're committed to living.

Erwin McManus

I literally have to remind myself all the time that being afraid of things going wrong isn't the way to make things go right.

Anonymous

If today were your last, would you do what you're doing?

Max Lucado

## For further reflection

Matthew 5:13-16; Deuteronomy 6:4-13;
Ephesians 4:17-32

## TODAY'S PRAYER

Thank you, Lord for this life! Help me to live it fully, and with gratitude for the gift that each day brings, sharing your love with all. Amen.

# Breathe

*Those who live in the shelter of the Most High will find rest in the shadow of the Almighty. This I declare about the LORD: He alone is my refuge, my place of safety; he is my God, and I trust him.*

PSALM 91:1-2

Finding peace in this chaotic world can be a challenge! Sometimes we just want to take a breather, a time out, and catch up with ourselves. The anxious feelings we get trying to plow through our to-do lists and everyday tasks can make us feel as though life is a treadmill—and we don't have access to the stop button!

Sometimes our anxiety can keep us from moving forward. It's like an invisible barrier that prevents us from doing what we need to do. It if not moving forward means we cannot accomplish a particular task, that creates more tension. (Even thinking about it creates anxiety!)

What if you could complete your tasks and responsibilities without fretting that you might not be able to get it all done? Take a breath. Recognize the challenge. Move forward. Avoiding a task creates a vortex which keeps you from your life. When you have a long task list, there will be stress, and there will be obstacles. However, when that task has been addressed you will experience relief—and confidence to do the next thing. One task at a time!

You don't need to have it all figured out to move forward.

Dale Partridge

If you can't fly, run; if you can't run, walk; if you can't walk, crawl; but by all means, keep moving.

Martin Luther King Jr.

## FOR FURTHER REFLECTION

Isaiah 35:3-7; Luke 12:22-32; Revelation 21:3-7

### TODAY'S PRAYER

Lord, you know how hard it is for me to move forward when my mind feels frozen in anxiety. I pray that you will bring peace and rest as I take on the challenges of this day, knowing that you are with me. Help me to rest in your presence while moving forward in your strength. I ask this in your name. Amen.

# Day 7

## Comforting Presence

*The Lord is my shepherd; I have all that I need. He lets me rest in green meadows; he leads me beside peaceful streams. He renews my strength. He guides me along right paths, bringing honor to his name. Even when I walk through the darkest valley, I will not be afraid, for you are close beside me. Your rod and your staff protect and comfort me. You prepare a feast for me in the presence of my enemies. You honor me by anointing my head with oil. My cup overflows with blessings. Surely your goodness and unfailing love will pursue me all the days of my life, and I will live in the house of the Lord forever.*

PSALM 23

This is probably the most familiar passage from the Bible. It is the inspired Word of God written through David, who was a shepherd who would become King. If you have dealt with fear and anxiety, you've probably memorized this passage and said it to yourself in times of need.

As a shepherd caring for a flock of sheep, David expresses his care and concern for the sheep in his fold. This is similar to how God cares for us. God is always present to provide, lead, and guide. His overwhelming love for us is comforting, and knowing he is with us can give us strength to face our days.

If you've never memorized this passage, begin today by writing it out. Then learn each verse of the psalm. As you commit this to memory, you will begin to recall this truth in times of struggle and in times of peace. What a gift to your heart and mind!

We have all things and abound; not because I have a good store of money in the bank, not because I have skill and wit with which to win my bread, but because "the Lord is my shepherd."

Charles Spurgeon

God walks with us. He scoops us up in His arms or simply sits with us in silent strength until we cannot avoid the awesome recognition that yes, even now, He is there.

Gloria Gaither

If we have not quiet in our own minds, all outward comforts will do no more good than a silken stocking to a scabbed leg; or a golden slipper to a gouty foot.

John Bunyan

## FOR FURTHER REFLECTION

Isaiah 43:1-5; John 1:1-5

### TODAY'S PRAYER

Lord, your presence is a comfort to me. Thank you for guiding my life and for the many blessings you have given to me. Amen.

# Day 8

## Strength for Today

*This is my command—be strong and courageous!*
*Do not be afraid or discouraged. For the Lord*
*your God is with you wherever you go.*

<small>Joshua 1:9</small>

Sometimes we need a little nudge, a hand to hold, or a shoulder to lean on. Worrying about a situation or relationship can dominate our thoughts and weaken our very heart. We ruminate over questions: How will things ever get better? Why did this happen? What can we do to fix it? Sometimes our thoughts and worries make us feel like we are actually doing something!

Have we asked the Lord about the things that weigh on our minds? Many times, the challenges in our lives that consume our thoughts prevent us from reaching out to God and to others for strength. We need to connect with God by sharing our hearts in prayer and reading the Word, as well as connecting with a trusted loved one who will share the burden.

One reason we resist asking for help is that we feel like nothing will help, or no one cares. These are lies to be challenged! Whatever struggle you are carrying, know that God will provide strength, courage, and an abiding presence—and also people who will be your support. Ask God today for what you need and know he will be faithful to provide!

His strength is perfect when our strength is gone. He'll carry us when we can't carry on. Raised in His power the weak become strong.

Jerry Salley and Steven Curtis Chapman

No one enjoys feeling weak, whether it is emotionally, spiritually or physically. There is something within the human spirit that wants to resist the thought of weakness. Many times this is nothing more than our human pride at work. Just as weakness carries a great potential for strength, pride carries an equally great potential for defeat.

Charles Stanley

## FOR FURTHER REFLECTION

1 Peter 5:6-7; Hebrews 13:6-9; Proverbs 18:10

## TODAY'S PRAYER

Lord Jesus, I bring you my troubles today knowing that you will provide strength for this day and courage to do what I can. Thank you for the people you have brought into my life to help me along the way. Amen.

# No Worries

*Turning to his disciples, Jesus said, "That is why
I tell you not to worry about everyday life—whether
you have enough food to eat or enough clothes to
wear. For life is more than food, and your body more
than clothing. Look at the ravens. They don't plant
or harvest or store food in barns, for God feeds them.
And you are far more valuable to him than any birds!
Can all your worries add a single moment to your
life? And if worry can't accomplish a little thing like
that, what's the use of worrying over bigger things?"*

LUKE 12:22-26

"No worries! Hakuna matata! It's all fine!"
These phrases can create tension when
we are struggling with life. If it only it
were that easy! As if just saying "don't worry" makes the
worry go away. Phrases like these can create shame and
frustration as we try to address the worry that fills our
minds.

Yet this is exactly what Jesus is telling us. Don't worry.
Jesus reminds us that God is taking care of the creation—
and we are cared for. Jesus also reminds us that worrying
isn't adding one moment to our lives. It is an exercise in
futility. But how can we make the choice not to worry?

Recognize when worrying is happening. For many people
it has become like background noise to our lives—a
constant presence in every moment, stealing precious
time. When you recognize your areas of worry, thank God

for how he will meet those needs. Begin to focus on this daily, moment by moment, to put into practice the peace that God offers!

If God be our God, He will give us peace in trouble. When there is a storm without, He will make peace within. The world can create trouble in peace, but God can create peace in trouble.

Thomas Watson

When life caves in, you do not need reasons—you need comfort. You do not need some answers—you need someone. And Jesus does not come to us with an explanation—He comes to us with His presence.

Bob Benson

## FOR FURTHER REFLECTION

Hebrews 12:1-12; Esther 4:13-17, 9:1; Psalm 139:7-12

### TODAY'S PRAYER

Thank you, God, that I can be confident in your care for me and my life! Help me to focus on your provision, be grateful for your faithfulness and live my life knowing how precious I am to you. Amen.

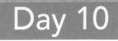

# Day 10

## Fixed on Truth

*And now, dear brothers and sisters, one final thing.
Fix your thoughts on what is true, and honorable,
and right, and pure, and lovely, and admirable.
Think about things that are excellent and worthy of
praise. Keep putting into practice all you learned and
received from me—everything you heard from me and
saw me doing. Then the God of peace will be with you.*

PHILIPPIANS 4:8-9

Sometimes when you feel anxious or fearful, your thoughts can swirl around the worst-case scenario and all the questions of what might happen. We fix our minds on the endless possibilities of what could go wrong, rather than what could go right. If you have experienced life at all, you know that things can go wrong sometimes—and awareness of that creates more fear and anxiety!

If all you do is keep a running list of all the things that could go bad, you will be overwhelmed. Instead of putting your head in the clouds or the sand, it's sensible to look at the risks or challenges in the situation you're facing. Consider what this passage of scripture says: Fix your thoughts on what is true, honorable, right, pure, lovely, admirable, excellent and worthy of praise. What a list! This will keep you from letting your anxious thoughts take over.

A time when you do not feel pressured by anxiety and fear is a good moment to practice refocusing your thoughts.

Remind yourself of something simple, like "God loves me" (true!) or "I am healthy" (and God is worthy of praise). Be creative—write them down as you put into practice fixing your thoughts.

If you worry, you are a worrier because your mind is saturated with worry thoughts. To counteract these, mark every passage in your Bible that speaks of faith, hope, and courage.

Norman Vincent Peale

Adversity is not a dead end but a detour to a better outcome than you can imagine!

Jon Gordon

Relying on God has to begin all over again every day, as if nothing had yet been done.

C. S. Lewis

## FOR FURTHER REFLECTION

Psalm 139:23-24; John 12:35-36;
2 Corinthians 1:1-11

### TODAY'S PRAYER

Lord, help me to fix my mind on the good in each situation, knowing that any difficulties are in your hands. I pray that my mind will be calmed knowing you are with me every day. Amen.

# Day 11

## Lifted Up

*In his kindness God called you to share in his
eternal glory by means of Christ Jesus. So after
you have suffered a little while, he will restore,
support, and strengthen you, and he will place
you on a firm foundation.*

1 PETER 5:10

Anxiety and fear are powerful emotions that can
totally rule—and potentially ruin—our lives. You
may have tried to rid yourself of these feelings,
but nothing seems to help. What would you say to letting
go of these feelings? Does it seem impossible?

Often, it is difficult to let go of things because we aren't
fully convinced that God is able to deal with the strong
feelings that control our lives. The creator of heaven and
earth has the power to do anything, yet we doubt. God's
ability to take on your troubles is greater than you know—
because if you did know, you would have given God all
your worries and fears a long time ago.

Realizing that God has more power than you do will
allow you to begin to surrender your cares to him. Today,
begin to release your worries to God, who cares for you
and will ease the weight of your worry.

God doesn't want us to be consumed with worry and anxiety. . . . He wants us to turn our worries over to Him, and to trust Him for the future.

Billy Graham

Worry is nothing but practical infidelity. The person who worries reveals his lack of trust in God and that he is trusting too much in self.

Lee Roberson

Worry is like racing the engine of an automobile without letting in the clutch.

Corrie ten Boom

## FOR FURTHER REFLECTION

Psalm 32; Luke 9:46-48; John 14:15-21

## TODAY'S PRAYER

Dear God, creator of heaven and earth, I ask humbly for you to take the worries and fears of my heart. Help me to trust you, knowing that you care for me and will handle anything in my life. Thank you for your love for me. Amen.

# Day 12

## Peace Be Still

*High waves were breaking into the boat, and it began
to fill with water. Jesus was sleeping at the back of the
boat with his head on a cushion. The disciples woke
him up, shouting, "Teacher, don't you care that we're
going to drown?" When Jesus woke up, he rebuked
the wind and said to the waves, "Silence! Be still!"
Suddenly the wind stopped, and there was a great
calm. Then he asked them, "Why are you afraid?
Do you still have no faith?"*

MARK 4:39-40

Do you ever feel like Jesus is asleep on the job?
There are storms in your life, and you are feeling
panicky wondering when he will show up and
take care of everything!

In this passage the disciples have been spending time with
Jesus, listening to him teach the crowds and explain in
depth about his lessons. What an amazing experience that
had to be!

Yet as they get into the boat with Jesus, a storm begins on
the lake and Jesus is asleep! The very men who just heard
him speak, the very men who have witnessed miracles,
are now doubting their safety—even with Jesus in the
boat. They even say, "Don't you care that we're going to
drown?"

You might be feeling this way today, wondering if Jesus
cares about the storm in your life. Don't drown in that
storm—call out to him and ask for help. Be assured that

he can calm the storm. Remembering times when Jesus has been faithful in your life, and what you have learned from him, will help you feel sure of his power to save. Will you ask Jesus today to calm your storm?

God never said that the journey would be easy, but he did say that the arrival would be worthwhile.

Max Lucado

The spirit of complaint is born out of an unwillingness to trust God with today . . . spending your time looking back toward Egypt or wishing for the future all the while missing what God is doing right now.

Priscilla Shirer

God is able to take the mess of our past and turn it into a message. He can take our trials and tests and turn them into a testimony.

Christine Caine

## For further reflection

Romans 5:1-11; Hebrews 6:18-20; Psalm 107

### TODAY'S PRAYER

Help, Lord! There are storms in my life that need calming. Guide me as I navigate through, and help me trust you, knowing you can provide great peace. Amen.

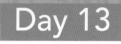

# Day 13

## Consolation

*Unless the Lord had given me help, I would soon*
*have dwelt in the silence of death. When I said,*
*"My foot is slipping," your unfailing love, Lord,*
*supported me. When anxiety was great within me,*
*your consolation brought me joy.*

PSALM 94:17-19 NIV

When anxiety and fear seem to be an ever-present reality, you can get weary. Well-meaning loved ones offer quick options to rid you of the constant chatter that drowns out the elusive peace you seek. And while some solutions are worth exploring there are others which create more fear of taking the risk to try again.

This passage describes so many of our experiences. We feel threatened by life or overwhelmed by circumstances. Yet read again where the psalmist cries out to God, "When I said,'My foot is slipping,' your unfailing love, Lord, supported me." It sounds simple—maybe too simple. Yet this is how we can receive consolation, which in turn brings joy.

Even if you have done this many times before, tell the Lord about it. What are you finding challenging? What is overwhelming your mind and heart? As you release these to the Lord, you will experience his support and consolation. It may not resolve whatever issue is troubling you, but it will provide you with relief and the clarity needed for resolution. We don't need to understand everything; God will open our minds and soften our hearts.

How sweet are the comforts of the Spirit! Who can muse upon eternal love, immutable purposes, covenant promises, finished redemption, the risen Saviour, his union with his people, the coming glory, and such like themes, without feeling his heart leaping with joy?

Charles Spurgeon

We can trust God with all our problems, all our heartaches, and especially with all our long-term anxieties. Every morning as we wake ourselves up with a splash of joy we can say, "WHATEVER, LORD!"

Barbara Johnson

Don't ever hesitate to take to God whatever is on your heart. He already knows it anyway, but He doesn't want you to bear its pain or celebrate its joy alone.

Billy Graham

## FOR FURTHER REFLECTION

Matthew 7:7-11; John 8:31-36; Philippians 3:10-14

## TODAY'S PRAYER

Lord Jesus, I am overwhelmed by
_____. I trust you to provide strength for me today. Amen.

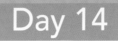

# Day 14

## Superpowers

*We can say with confidence, "The Lord is my helper,
so I will have no fear. What can mere people
do to me?"*

Hebrews 13:6

Do you have a cape? You know—the kind that superheroes wear? Maybe your cape looks like a bath towel or a scarf tied around your neck. Or perhaps you hung up yours a long time ago. You forgot about the power of the Lord working in your life.

Sometimes this happens after we experience a devastating loss and cannot imagine where we will draw strength from for the day ahead. Other times we forget the Lord's power in our life because we don't access it day to day—we leave that for our weekly church service. At one time or another, many of us have simply felt powerless to change our circumstances.

The Lord Jesus is working in your life. For real. That's a powerful thought. What would be different in your life if you felt confident that the Lord is with you? You have been through many things and Jesus was with you every minute. Even in the most desperate days, the Lord has provided strength for you to get through to today. Remember to put on your cape today by spending some time with Jesus, who will provide all the power you need to move through this day.

Many Christians estimate difficulty in the light of their own resources, and thus they attempt very little; and they always fail. All giants have been weak men who did great things for God because they relied on His power and presence to be with them.

Hudson Taylor

It is for us to pray not for tasks equal to our powers, but for powers equal to our tasks, to go forward with a great desire forever beating at the door of our hearts as we travel toward our distant goal.

Helen Keller

Prayer is a weapon. Therapy is a strategy.

Dr. Anita Phillips

## FOR FURTHER REFLECTION

Philippians 4:11-14; 1 Timothy 4:7-16;
2 Chronicles 32:7-8

## TODAY'S PRAYER

Lord Jesus, thank you for your strength. Help me to grow in my faith that you are always with me and will help me with my challenges. Amen.

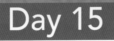

# Day 15

## Change the Story

*God has not given us a spirit of fear and timidity,
but of power, love, and self-discipline.*

2 TIMOTHY 1:7

How do you describe yourself? Extrovert, introvert, athletic, creative, shy? Who you think you are plays a big part in how you go about your life in the world. You may be thinking of times you were "told" who you were by family, school friends—or worse, bullies. Other people sometimes give us identities that may be incorrect.

If the story we tell ourselves *about* ourselves is inaccurate, we should begin to change it. If your story doesn't reflect what God says about you, it may be creating fear and anxieties in your life. Do you feel "less than," or "damaged," or "too far gone" to be fully loved and accepted by God and others?

An old story that's on repeat in your head can keep you from living life the way God intended—which is to live it free. When fear and anxiety rule our thoughts, we need to recognize what our brain is telling us and then recognize it isn't based in truth. God loves you, cares for you and has a purpose for your life. As you begin to put this on repeat, you will begin to experience God's love which will bring you peace of heart and mind.

Though our feelings come and go, His love for us does not.

C. S. Lewis

The man who is not afraid to admit everything that he sees to be wrong with himself, and yet recognizes that he may be the object of God's love precisely because of his shortcomings, can begin to be sincere. His sincerity is based on confidence, not in his own illusions about himself, but in the endless, unfailing mercy of God.

Thomas Merton

Who gave mercy my address? Or told it how to get to my room? . . . Without asking me my permission a good God had come to my rescue.

Jackie Hill Perry

## FOR FURTHER REFLECTION

Psalm 17; Luke 12:6-8; Romans 8:31-39

### TODAY'S PRAYER

Thank you, God for loving me. Help me to live and walk in your love for me and the power of your Holy Spirit! Amen.

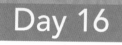

# Fear Not

*Be strong and courageous! Do not be afraid
and do not panic before them. For the L*ORD
*your God will personally go ahead of you.
He will neither fail you nor abandon you.*

DEUTERONOMY 31:6

When we are feeling overcome by a situation, our minds race. We try to figure out how it will turn out, or what we should do. Often, we imagine ourselves alone and without resources, which can make us freeze instead of taking action to resolve the issue.

You are not alone, ever. While you may not have a human ally who you can count on in a particular challenge, God will always be with you! We can know that the Lord will go before us and will not leave us. That fact alone can bring peace.

We are made to be in relationship with God and people. At times, our fear and anxiety prevent us from making these life-giving connections. You might feel disconnected from God and doubt his presence. Reconnect with God and begin to experience his presence. Your relationship with God is based on his love for you and your acceptance of this truth. He is with you as you go through your life and in all the challenges you face!

Many people believe in God, yet they don't live in relationship with God. Through reading his Word, prayer, and connection with other believers, we can begin to experience the peace that overcomes our fear. Begin to experience the comfort of God's presence.

God, who is everywhere, never leaves us. Yet he seems sometimes to be present, sometimes absent. If we do not know Him well, we do not realize that he may be more present to us when he is absent than when he is present.

Thomas Merton

The most holy and necessary practice in our spiritual life is the presence of God.

Brother Lawrence

Faith is not believing in my own unshakable belief. Faith is believing an unshakable God when everything in me trembles and quakes.

Beth Moore

## FOR FURTHER REFLECTION

2 Corinthians 12:8-10; Philippians 1:3-6;
1 Timothy 4:10

### TODAY'S PRAYER

Thank you, God, for your mighty presence! Help me to see you more clearly. Help me trust you as I face the challenges of my life. Amen.

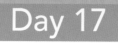
# Next Steps

*When I am afraid, I will put my trust in you.*

PSALM 56:3

Sometimes, to feel a sense of peace we need to know what to do. We are eager for someone to tell us the details of how to do what needs to be done, someone we trust. Here's the challenge: most of the time, life doesn't have step-by-step instructions! The unknown is where insecurities and fears show up.

This passage is a "next step" you can trust. Awareness that you feel afraid or insecure is your cue to put your trust in God. While this may seem simplistic, it is the path to freedom. The path takes more than one step, but eventually your faith and trust in God will bring the peace for which you long.

Today, choose to trust God—especially if you are not feeling afraid of anything. It is during those times that you will build your faith for the times of testing. This isn't to suggest you will completely remove fear from your life, but it does mean that even when you do feel afraid, you will know who you can trust with your life.

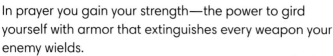

In prayer you gain your strength—the power to gird yourself with armor that extinguishes every weapon your enemy wields.

Priscilla Shirer

Past boldness is no assurance of future boldness. Boldness demands continual reliance on God's spirit.

Andy Stanley

The presence of fear does not mean you have no faith. Fear visits everyone. But make your fear a visitor and not a resident.

Max Lucado

## FOR FURTHER REFLECTION

Joshua 1:6-9; 1 Kings 3:6-14; John 3:16-21;
1 Timothy 6:11-16

## TODAY'S PRAYER

Lord Jesus, help me to be aware of your strength and love for me each and every day. You are always faithful. Help me as I rest in your promises. Amen.

# What's Love Got to Do with It?

*Perfect love expels all fear. If we are afraid, it is for fear of punishment, and this shows that we have not fully experienced his perfect love.*

1 JOHN 4:18

There is an old Tina Turner song with the title "What's Love Got to Do with It?"—a rather sad song about relationships that are purely physical. Many of us struggle to understand our relationship with God because we want it to be more in the physical realm than spiritual. In our moments of fear and anxiety, we really want to actually see him.

Yet God is there. God is in the embrace of a loved one who is walking the journey with you. His presence is in his Word, the scriptures that tell of God's faithfulness through all time. God is seen in nature—the beauty of the flowers, the changing of the seasons, and the power in the storms all speak to his mighty presence and care for the creation. God's love for you is felt as you meditate on the scriptures, focus on gratitude for all you have, and center your thoughts on him.

God's love is perfect for you. It is full of grace and mercy. It embraces you and your imperfections, encouraging you to fully accept the love that will strengthen you for your life! Seek to fully understand God's love in your life. Seek to know it more than anything else you know!

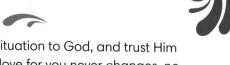

Learn to commit every situation to God, and trust Him for the outcome. God's love for you never changes, no matter what problems you face or how unsettled life becomes.

Billy Graham

We must never take our relationship with God for granted, become complacent, and lose the wonder of His love for us.

David Jeremiah

When one has once fully entered the realm of love, the world—no matter how imperfect—becomes rich and beautiful, for it consists solely of opportunities for love.

Søren Kierkegaard

## FOR FURTHER REFLECTION

Isaiah 40:27-31; 1 Corinthians 13:1-7; Psalm 121

### TODAY'S PRAYER

Thank you, God for loving me! Help me live each day experiencing your presence. I want to share your love with others as you have freely given love to me! Amen.

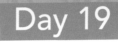

# Never Alone

*"Do not be afraid, for I have ransomed you. I have
called you by name; you are mine. When you go
through deep waters, I will be with you. When you
go through rivers of difficulty, you will not drown.
When you walk through the fire of oppression, you
will not be burned up; the flames will not consume
you. For I am the Lord, your God, the Holy One
of Israel, your Savior."*

Isaiah 43:1-3

Anxiety and fear can create isolation, as you may
know personally. When these feelings invade our
minds, it can block us from recognizing God's
presence or welcoming the support of loved ones who
are there to lean on. The feelings become like a cage that
keeps us from experiencing peace in our trials.

Take a minute right now to think about the places and
trials God has brought you through. If the voice of
anxiety and fear is loud in your mind today, you might
have trouble coming up with many things. If you woke
up this morning, thank God. If you have a roof over your
head, food to eat, clothes to wear, clean water to drink,
you can thank God.

When we direct our minds to the way God has met our
needs, it prepares us to trust him to carry us through
times of trial in the future. Notice that the passage from
Isaiah doesn't say "if" you go through deep waters or "if"
you walk through the fires of oppression. It says "when,"

which means that God knows what is ahead of you and will be present with you throughout your life. Make time today to focus on how God has been there for you.

If I were going to begin practicing the presence of God for the first time today, it would help to begin by admitting the three most terrible truths of our existence: that we are so ruined, and so loved, and in charge of so little.

Anne Lamott

You know people just assume, well, all my life I'll be a worrier. That doesn't have to be true. There's a way to drink from God's presence so much that worry begins to dissipate.

Max Lucado

Vision is the ability to see God's presence, to perceive God's power, to focus on God's plan in spite of the obstacles.

Chuck Swindoll

## FOR FURTHER REFLECTION

Ephesians 2:4-10; Zephaniah 3:16-20; 1 John 3:1-3

### TODAY'S PRAYER

Lord, help me see you as I search for you. Thank you for the blessing of your presence! Amen.

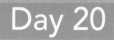

# Day 20

## Encouragement for Today

*Worry weighs a person down; an encouraging word cheers a person up.*

<small>PROVERBS 12:25</small>

The definition of encouragement is "the action of giving someone support, confidence, or hope." Here's some encouragement for you today—you are loved and fully accepted by God!

When you are burdened by "what if's" or "if only's," when relationships or loved ones are causing concern, if your financial situation is shaky, here's what will lift those burdens: the truth that God loves you and is for you. You might wonder, "What does God loving me have to do with my struggles? How can that make any difference?"

When we know and believe that God loves us and accepts us, that fact becomes the foundation of our lives. This allows us to deal with the struggles of each day from a place of security and strength, confident that God will provide for us in any situation we face. We do not have to carry the weight of the world alone.

This is a big shift in thinking for many people. Some find it hard to believe that God could love them after all they have done. Others may not "feel" like God loves them—based on a feeling, rather than the truth. God loves you and knows you. He created you and has a purpose and plan for your life. Focus on this today and experience support, confidence, and hope from the God of the Universe.

Define yourself as one radically loved by God. This is the true self. Every other identity is illusion.

Brennan Manning

When we talk about the peace of God, don't think of singing and swaying and holding hands in a circle. The peace of God is strong, intense, palpable, real. You can sense its stable presence giving you inner security despite insecure circumstances.

Priscilla Shirer

Disappointment and failure are not signs that God has forsaken you or stopped loving you. The devil wants you to believe God no longer loves you, but it isn't true. God's love for us never fails.

Billy Graham

## FOR FURTHER REFLECTION

2 Corinthians 5:16-17; Ephesians 2:8-10;
Romans 8:1-4

### TODAY'S PRAYER

Thank you, God, for loving me just as I am. Help me, Lord, to receive this truth and live my life in your strength and hope. Amen.

# Day 21

## Stay Present

*Don't worry about tomorrow, for tomorrow will bring
its own worries. Today's trouble is enough for today.*

Matthew 6:34

How much of your life are you missing because you are either thinking about your past or worried about your future? Does your thinking distract you from truly experiencing what is happening around you right now? Often our fear and anxiety keep us from the joys of life.

If you can relate to this, you may have some sense of how it works. Past experiences and trauma can keep us in the past—and on high alert for what can possibly go wrong in the future. There are varying degrees of this, and some become so numbing and debilitating that individuals essentially check out of their lives.

One practice to "stay present" uses our five senses: sight, smell, touch, hearing, taste. It sounds simple but it is powerful. Take a moment and notice something from each of the senses where you are right this moment. What do you see? Smell? Touch? Taste? Hear?

If you struggle with distraction and a focus on negative things, it will be helpful to ask for help from a therapist, pastor, or friend. Our minds are powerful, and past traumas and experiences can prevent us from full involvement in the present. Reach out today and find healing for your life.

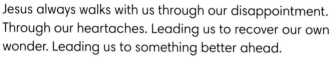

Jesus always walks with us through our disappointment. Through our heartaches. Leading us to recover our own wonder. Leading us to something better ahead.

Christine Caine

I've had a lot of worries in my life, most of which never happened.

Mark Twain

Set a clear focus in your life , and fear will be crowded out. The more you fix your eyes on God's purpose for you, the more you will overcome your fear.

David Jeremiah

## FOR FURTHER REFLECTION

Psalm 18:1-6; Hebrews 4:14-16; Revelation 3:19-20

## TODAY'S PRAYER

Thank you, Lord, for this moment in my life. Help me to find peace in this moment, knowing you are always with me. Amen.

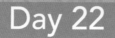

# Help Is on the Way!

*Say to those with fearful hearts, "Be strong, and do not fear, for your God is coming to destroy your enemies. He is coming to save you."*

Isaiah 35:4

When things in our life are scary—say, a diagnosis we weren't looking for, or a relationship challenge, or facing our own sinful choices—it can be difficult to move forward. We can feel alone and isolated, unable to find the strength to deal with the day ahead.

Remember this: you are not alone . . . ever. God is merciful and will provide strength for you for every step of your life. No matter what the situation, when fear begins to rise up in you, recall how God has been faithful in the past.

You don't have to fix the whole situation at once. That idea is another way fear keeps us trapped. When we are fearful, we may believe the lie that we have to have an answer completely figured out before we can move on.

Whatever is causing you to fear today, know that God will provide his strength and is coming to save you. It may look different than what you expect, but be confident that God is with you!

God has promised that His grace will be given according to our need and that not only will we survive by the skin of our teeth, if we trust Him and hang on to Him for dear life—grieving, yes, but as those who have hope—we will also thrive again.

Beth Moore

Love is what carries you, for it is always there, even in the dark, or most in the dark, but shining out at times like gold stitches in a piece of embroidery.

Wendell Berry

Faith is a living, daring confidence in God's grace, so sure and certain that the believer would stake his life on it a thousand times.

Martin Luther

## FOR FURTHER REFLECTION

Psalm 34:4-10; Matthew 8:23-27; John 14:27

## TODAY'S PRAYER

Lord, thank you for giving me your strength to face my fears. Help me as I fight the fear that wants to control my life. Amen.

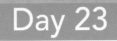

# Day 23

## Light for Our Life

*The LORD is my light and my salvation—so why should
I be afraid? The LORD is my fortress, protecting me
from danger, so why should I tremble?*

PSALM 27:1

Many children are afraid of the dark. Their imaginations can create all kinds of monsters from the shapes of furniture, toys, and clothing thrown on the back of a chair. The shadows and outlines create images that look harmless when the light is on. As we become adults, we are able to discern those images and go back to sleep.

But sometimes as adults we imagine the worst possible situation about things in our life that we haven't yet exposed to the Light. When we are able to hold our struggles and fears up to the Light of God's Word, prayer, and connection with other believers, we are able to discern what is true. It doesn't mean that we won't have feelings about these things—but we will know that God is with us as we go through them.

Whatever fear you may be facing today, offer it to the Light of the Lord. Ask God to reveal the truth, provide grace to handle what you need to, and give you strength to take the necessary steps to move forward. Talk with a trusted friend. Sometimes that can be the most difficult part, sharing out loud what is buried in your heart, yet it can offer a different view on whatever you are carrying alone. Search the scriptures to see more of the truth about the Lord's provision for your life. It's time to turn on the Light!

Faith is seeing light with your heart when all your eyes see is darkness.

Barbara Johnson

We can easily forgive a child who is afraid of the dark; the real tragedy of life is when men are afraid of the light.

Plato

Darkness cannot drive out darkness; only light can do that. Hate cannot drive out hate; only love can do that.

Martin Luther King Jr.

## FOR FURTHER REFLECTION

John 8:12; 1 John 1:5-7; 2 Peter 1:16-21

## TODAY'S PRAYER

Lord God, shed your light on my fears so that I may discern your truth and have courage and wisdom for whatever I face today. Amen.

# Day 24

## Can You Believe It?

*When they saw him walking on the water, they cried*
*out in terror, thinking he was a ghost. They were all*
*terrified when they saw him. But Jesus spoke to them*
*at once. "Don't be afraid," he said. "Take courage!*
*I am here!" Then he climbed into the boat, and the*
*wind stopped. They were totally amazed.*

MARK 6:49-51

In this passage of scripture, the disciples have been with Jesus, watching him teach, heal, and perform the miracle of feeding 5,000 people with two fish and five loaves of bread. Jesus sends the disciples on their way by boat and stays back on the shore to pray. When a storm comes up, Jesus walks towards them on the water!

In the midst of our fears, it can feel like the storm will overtake us. We fear what will happen as the storm rages. And when help arrives, in whatever form—a check in the mail, a phone call from a loved one, or an opportunity that was totally out of the blue—we cannot believe it!

Yet our faith tells us that Jesus is always willing to be in the boat with us. He comes to calm our fears and offer strength. Our challenge is to believe that Jesus will provide exactly what we need for whatever storm we are experiencing. Our belief needs to start before the storm, by taking notice of how Jesus provided for those he served—and how he has also provided for you. Today, look for Jesus walking towards you in the midst of your storm and saying, "Don't be afraid! Take courage! I am here!"

Fear can keep you up all night, but faith makes one fine pillow.

Phillip Gulley

Nothing on earth compares to the strength God is willing to interject into lives caught in the act of believing.

Beth Moore

Because God is with you all the time, no place is any closer to God than the place where you are right now.

Rick Warren

## FOR FURTHER REFLECTION

Proverbs 3:5-6; Hebrews 11; Mark 11:22-24

### TODAY'S PRAYER

Thank you, Jesus, for your faithfulness to me! Help me to recognize that you are always with me and will provide strength and hope for my journey. Amen.

# Surrender

*Give your burdens to the LORD, and he will take care of you. He will not permit the godly to slip and fall.*

PSALM 55:22

One of the most difficult things to do when you are feeling anxious is to let go of the thing you are worried about. Anxiety actually is more about control than anything else. You feel out of control when you are feeling anxious--not in control. There is little in life that we do control, and so when the unexpected comes, we begin to focus on what could go wrong, what could help, what should have happened, etc.

What would it be like to surrender those thoughts and concerns to the Lord? You may have already been in prayer about the issue, you may have connected with a trusted friend, and you may have already talked to a counselor—but what about surrendering to God all of these worries?

It may seem impossible to hand over your concerns to the Lord. If he had it under control, you wouldn't be worried, right?! Well, the truth is that God cares about your concerns and your life. The decision to give your worries to the Lord is a daily choice, sometimes hourly! It is a practice and discipline which will bring you peace. God promises to care for you. Make the choice to surrender to him today.

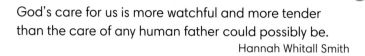

God's care for us is more watchful and more tender than the care of any human father could possibly be.

Hannah Whitall Smith

Instead of worrying, we're to thank God for his promise to work everything together for good, trusting in his sovereign grace.

Randy Alcorn

Greater is Thy care for me than all the care I can exercise over myself.

Thomas à Kempis

## For further reflection

James 1:5-8; Hebrews 12:1-2; Psalm 37:5-6

## TODAY'S PRAYER

Lord God, today I am handing over my worries to you. I know you will provide an answer and loving care for me. Amen.

# Day 26

## Comfort and Care

*Jesus said, "Come to me, all of you who are weary
and carry heavy burdens, and I will give you rest.
Take my yoke upon you. Let me teach you, because
I am humble and gentle at heart, and you will find
rest for your souls. For my yoke is easy to bear,
and the burden I give you is light."*

MATTHEW 11:28-30

What a great invitation Jesus offers you in this passage of scripture! There are days when we are so overwhelmed by the worries of our life that we need someone to be there for us, and Jesus offers this to you.

So, what does it look like to go to Jesus and let him carry your burdens? It can be hard to lean into Jesus when you feel weighed down by the cares in your life. Some of the ways we go to him are to read the Bible, pray, and connect with loved ones. As you read the Bible you will be reminded of God's promises to you. As you pray and express your concerns to the Lord, he will hear you! And as we connect with others who love us, we will experience the care of the Lord. In a gentle way, Jesus will teach you a new way of life, and provides rest for you.

Take a deep breath (or three) and re-read this passage. Spend some time praying. Ask Jesus to take your burdens. Rest in the fact that he is faithful. We need to do this every day. As concerns come to your mind, offer them to Jesus. Remind yourself of Christ's loving care and concern for you and your life. It will become your way of life, and bring the peace that surpasses understanding.

We can choose to gather to our hearts the thorns of disappointment, failure, loneliness, and dismay due to our present situation, or we can gather the flowers of God's grace, unbounding love, abiding presence, and unmatched joy.

Barbara Johnson

God is the God of "right now." He doesn't want you sitting around regretting yesterday. Nor does He want you wringing your hands and worrying about the future. He wants you focusing on what He is saying to you and putting in front of you . . . right now.

Priscilla Shirer

You don't have to be alone in your hurt! Comfort is yours. Joy is an option. And it's all been made possible by your Savior. He went without comfort so you might have it. He postponed joy so you might share in it. He willingly chose isolation so you might never be alone in your hurt and sorrow.

Joni Eareckson Tada

## FOR FURTHER REFLECTION

Deuteronomy 31:6-8; John 16:22-24; Psalm 32:7-11

## TODAY'S PRAYER

Thank you, Lord, for your comfort and care for me. Help me to trust you more, and to know that you go before me and will provide the strength I need for my life. Amen.

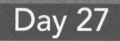

# Always and Forever

*Can anything ever separate us from Christ's love?*
*Does it mean he no longer loves us if we have trouble*
*or calamity, or are persecuted, or hungry, or destitute,*
*or in danger, or threatened with death? . . . No,*
*despite all these things, overwhelming victory*
*is ours through Christ, who loved us.*

ROMANS 8:35, 37

The overwhelming love of Christ is always and forever with us. Despite anything we may face in life, the presence of his love in our lives provides the strength we need.

Are you dealing with something that causes you to doubt God's love for you? Perhaps it is a choice you made, and the consequences are harsh. Maybe you are experiencing hardships and wonder where God is in all of the struggle. These are not uncommon feelings. When life isn't all rosy, we doubt the love we are promised in Christ.

The truth is that in this world we will have difficult experiences and relationships. The blessing is that Christ has overcome this world because of his great love for us. We can experience peace and freedom even in the middle of the mess! While we are here on earth, we have to believe in the love of Christ—which is always and forever with us.

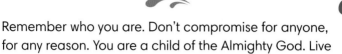

Remember who you are. Don't compromise for anyone, for any reason. You are a child of the Almighty God. Live that truth.

Lysa TerKeurst

The greater your knowledge of the goodness and grace of God on your life, the more likely you are to praise Him in the storm.

Matt Chandler

God proved His love on the Cross. When Christ hung, and bled, and died, it was God saying to the world—"I love you."

Billy Graham

## FOR FURTHER REFLECTION

John 15:9-17; 1 Chronicles 16:34-36; Psalm 66:16-20

### TODAY'S PRAYER

Thank you, Jesus, for your great and unfailing love for me! I want to be confident in you when life brings challenges. Remind me of your love in my desperation and in my daily walk. In your powerful name, amen.

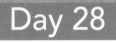

# Handrails

*Let us hold tightly without wavering to the hope we
affirm, for God can be trusted to keep his promise.*

HEBREWS 10:23

When we are nervous about a situation, it would be helpful if there were handrails to grab onto! If you have a fear of heights, you definitely would want to know there is a railing that will prevent you from going over the edge. We have similar feelings about the challenges in our lives that do not come with instructions—we need help!

Where do you look for help when fear and worry want to take command of the situation? They want to be in the driver's seat and take you away from your desired destination. It's in times like these we need to reach for and grasp God's hand. How do we do that when we can't actually, physically touch his hand? By prayer, reading the Bible, and reaching out to someone who will help you walk through the challenging times.

God is faithful and will provide what you need, whatever the situation. Your trust in him begins before times of trial, as you build your relationship with God. Then when times of trial come, you will recognize his provision. God can be trusted no matter what we face! We can be confident in this promise.

Hope is called the anchor of the soul (Hebrews 6:19), because it gives stability to the Christian life. But hope is not simply a "wish" (I wish that such-and-such would take place); rather, it is that which latches on to the certainty of the promises of the future that God has made.

R. C. Sproul

Never be afraid to trust an unknown future to a known God.

Corrie ten Boom

We choose what attitudes we have right now. And it's a continuing choice.

John C. Maxwell

## For further reflection

Psalm 42; 1 Corinthians 10:12-13; Isaiah 41:9-10

### TODAY'S PRAYER

Heavenly Father, thank you for your faithful help in my times of need! I know I can trust you and can rest in your promises. Amen.

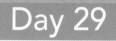

# Day 29

## Stressed Out

*In my distress I prayed to the Lord, and the Lord answered me and set me free. The Lord is for me, so I will have no fear. What can mere people do to me?*

PSALM 118:5-6

Feeling stressed out? Do your family responsibilities feel way too busy, or are you short on time to complete a project at work? Stress eats away at us—and yet *some* stress is good for us. It seems strange, but it is true! Stress is the way we strengthen our bodies. Exercise stresses the systems of our body as we work out and develops our strength and stamina. Exercise is a natural stress reliever, too. However, some of us feel stress just thinking about a workout!

What do you do when you are stressed? Fear and anxiety can arise from too much stress that goes without resolution. As we carry our worries and our fear of the unknown, we can begin to accept the experience of stress as a normal way of life.

Stop for a minute and take a deep breath. Whatever is stressing you out right now, God already knows how it will turn out. Will you sit for a while and share with God in prayer all of the stressful things you are dealing with? Whatever the situation, God is not stressed about it at all! God loves you and wants to offer you his strength and wisdom for each day of your life.

Get alone with Jesus, and He will comfort your hearts, and restore your weary souls.

Charles Spurgeon

One is given strength to bear what happens to one, but not the one hundred and one different things that might happen.

C. S. Lewis

May God remind us daily—no matter what kind of obstacles we face—that we are loved and empowered by the One who brought the universe into existence with the mere sound of His voice. Nothing is impossible for Him.

Beth Moore

## FOR FURTHER REFLECTION

Psalm 94:12-19; Matthew 11:28-30; John 14:1-4

## TODAY'S PRAYER

Dear Jesus, I need relief today from the stress in my life. You are greater than all these things that occupy my mind. Thank you for the assurance that you are able to guide me and strengthen me as I work through to victory. Amen.

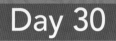

# Trust God

*Fearing people is a dangerous trap,*
*but trusting the LORD means safety.*

PROVERBS 29:25

Some of our fears are "people based." Many of us have folks in our life who are demanding or who bully others with their words or behavior. Some of us are dealing with trauma from a past relationship. Maybe right now there is a threatening person in your life—if so, please reach out for help today.

When we begin to feel that the world is a bit too "peopley," we begin to withdraw. It's too difficult to deal with their attitudes, demands and behaviors—we long for the quiet that our solitude brings. However, too much solitude can become a pit. We were created for relationships, and when we are in healthy ones we can experience life the way God designed us to.

If you have found yourself isolated and the thought of connecting with another person brings stress, take a step towards a safe person. Ask God for help and direction to find a way to begin to connect with someone. Someone needs you in their life, too. There will always be someone who you can begin to share life with. It doesn't have to be a crowd of people. Jesus shared his life on earth with a small group, and look how that changed the world!

The next best thing to being wise oneself is to live in a circle of those who are.

C. S. Lewis

I think it is interesting that God designed people to need other people. We see those cigarette advertisements with the rugged cowboy riding around alone on a horse, and we think that is strength, when really, it is like setting your soul down on a couch and not exercising it. The soul needs to interact with other people to be healthy.

Donald Miller

It may not be an easy thing to live in sweet fellowship with all those with whom we come in contact; but that is why the grace of God is given to us.

D. L. Moody

## FOR FURTHER REFLECTION

Matthew 4:18-22; Acts 2:42-47; Proverbs 17:17

### TODAY'S PRAYER

Thank you, Lord, for your friendship with me! I know you have created me for connection. Please help me as I connect with others. Amen.

# Eternal Hope!

*When I saw him, I fell at his feet as if I were dead.*
*But he laid his right hand on me and said, "Don't be*
*afraid! I am the First and the Last. I am the living*
*one. I died, but look—I am alive forever and ever!*
*And I hold the keys of death and the grave."*

REVELATION 1:17-18

Our faith journey is unique to each of us. We came to faith in Jesus Christ through many different churches, traditions, and people who carried the message of the gospel. Some of you may not be sure whether you really believe Jesus died and rose again, or even if he is the son of God. Others may have a solid faith in Jesus, but because of some of the traditions, churches and people along their faith journey they may live in fear that if they do something wrong Christ will reject them.

The good news of Jesus Christ is that you can be saved from living apart from God. Your faith in Christ can bring you peace and assurance that God is always with you. If you are living in fear of not being accepted by Christ, you can change that today by accepting his love, grace, and mercy. If you already have given your life to Christ and believe him to be the son of God, yet you are still living in fear, ask the Lord today to reveal his truth to you and bring you peace.

Christ died and rose again so you can experience freedom! If your past makes it hard for you to experience that freedom, connect today with someone and talk about your faith. Join a Bible study and begin to know the truth that will set you free. Being confident of your salvation will begin to calm your fears. You will learn to live your life in close relationship with God, and know you will never be rejected.

The roaring thunder of the law and the fear of the terror of judgment are both used to bring us to Christ, but the final victory culminating in our salvation is won through God's loving-kindness.

Charles Spurgeon

Saving us is the greatest and most concrete demonstration of God's love, the definitive display of His grace throughout time and eternity.

David Jeremiah

Faith is not believing in my own unshakable belief. Faith is believing an unshakable God when everything in me trembles and quakes.

Beth Moore

## For further reflection

Romans 10:9-10; John 3:15-21; John 5:24-30

### TODAY'S PRAYER

Lord, I believe that Jesus Christ is the Savior of the world, and that he died and rose again to forgive my sins. I receive your grace by faith. Thank you for my eternal salvation. Amen.

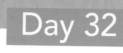

# Have Faith

*Jesus overheard them and said to Jairus,*
*"Don't be afraid. Just have faith."*

MARK 5:36

Many editions of the Bible have "red letters" for the passages where Jesus spoke. It is amazing that the words of Christ have survived centuries and languages! Jesus' words still have powerful impact today around the world—and yet they are so very personal to each of us.

The miracles of Jesus are amazing evidence of his power. We read, though, that many times, the disciples doubted him even though they saw the miracles firsthand! Jesus' power is still working miracles today—you may have experienced something amazing in your life!

Yet we still worry, and we are still frequently afraid that situations won't turn out as we expect or hope. In our lives on this planet we will experience heartache and disappointments. However, Jesus says, "Don't be afraid. Just have faith." In what situation in your life today would these "red letter" words of Jesus bring comfort to you? Ask Jesus today to strengthen your faith!

Even if people have disappointed you or circumstances have not turned out as you had hoped or prayed, know that God is with you, cares for you, and loves you. He is working all these things together for your good right at this very moment.

Christine Caine

The Christian life is not a constant high. I have my moments of deep discouragement. I have to go to God in prayer with tears in my eyes, and say, "O God, forgive me, or help me."

Billy Graham

I will not fear, for you are ever with me, and you will never leave me to face my perils alone.

Thomas Merton

## For further reflection

1 John 4:4-8; Isaiah 40; Psalm 91

### TODAY'S PRAYER

Thank you, Jesus, for your miraculous power at work in my life. Help me be encouraged in whatever situation may feel overwhelming to me. I trust you. Amen.

# God's Delight

*The LORD your God is living among you. He is*
*a mighty savior. He will take delight in you with*
*gladness. With his love, he will calm all your fears.*
*He will rejoice over you with joyful songs.*

ZEPHANIAH 3:17

What is on your mind today? What is filling your thoughts: concerns, challenges, regrets? Maybe you have become numb because something happened to you or to someone you love that was so awful you just cannot believe it. Life can be challenging, and the messages of the world will fill our thoughts with doubt and fear.

In the midst of our worries and fears, how encouraging it is to remember that the God of the universe, the Creator of all things, takes delight in us! He will calm our fears and will sing joyful songs over us. God is with us, nearer than we realize, in every minute of every day. His love is ever present, and when we recognize this truth it will bring peace.

Begin to focus on this passage and meditate on the fact that God delights in you, loves you, and will calm your fears. This will fill your mind with truth that will transform the way you deal with your worries and fears. Some situations may still trigger difficult emotions, but you will have greater assurance that God is near and will provide peace.

The great secret of the Christian life is to begin experiencing God as He desires me to experience Him. God's greatest delight is to bring me into His presence.

A. W. Tozer

If you find yourself right now in a place where you are heartbroken, I want to remind you that Christ is very close to the broken. Our culture throws broken things away, but our Savior never does. He gently gathers all the pieces, and with His love and in His time, He puts us back together.

Sheila Walsh

My prayer today is that we will feel the loving arms of God wrapped around us and will know in our hearts that He will never forsake us as we trust in Him.

Billy Graham

## FOR FURTHER REFLECTION

Isaiah 62:3-5; Psalm 18; Genesis 1:31

### TODAY'S PRAYER

Thank you, God, for delighting in me, for loving me, and for being an ever-present help for me. Help me to remember that you are always with me. Amen.

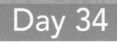

# God's Promise

*The LORD says, "I will rescue those who love me. I will*
*protect those who trust in my name. When they call*
*on me, I will answer; I will be with them in trouble.*
*I will rescue and honor them. I will reward them*
*with a long life and give them my salvation."*

PSALM 91:14-16

When we are afraid or anxious, we want assurance that everything will be alright. Many times, when we share our concerns with someone they will try to encourage us by saying, "Everything will be alright." (We usually don't believe it!)

When our concerns dominate our thoughts, it's hard to believe that things will all work out. We defend our anxious, fearful belief, and find it hard to listen to other options. Yet the very things we need are calm reassurance and the ability to trust that it *will* all work out.

God's promise in this passage is pretty clear. He is with us, working out whatever trouble we are experiencing. He will rescue us. What are you believing about your situation? Does it seem like God is not fulfilling his promise to rescue you? God's timing is perfect, but as humans we can't quite grasp what takes God so long. Yet this is what the promise says: when we call on him, he will be with us in our trouble. What do you need to call on God for today?

God's hand never slips. He never makes a mistake. His every move is for our own good and for our ultimate good.

Billy Graham

Sometimes God lets you be in a situation that only He can fix so that you can see that He is the One who fixes it. Rest. He's got it.

Tony Evans

Backtrack and remember all the places God has been so faithful before in your life. Then go forward with assurance and confidence He is the same faithful God.

Lysa TerKeurst

## FOR FURTHER REFLECTION

John 16:33; Isaiah 41:10; Psalm 37:23-24

### TODAY'S PRAYER

Heavenly Father, thank you for your loving care for me. Strengthen my faith in you. I know you are always working in my life for my good. That brings me peace. Amen.

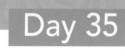
# Get a Grip!

*I hold you by your right hand—I, the L*ORD *your God.*
*And I say to you, 'Don't be afraid.*
*I am here to help you.'"*

ISAIAH 41:13

Have you ever been so anxious about a situation that someone told you to "get a grip"? It probably didn't feel very helpful or comforting, and it certainly didn't help you feel better in that moment. Yet there are many times when we recognize there is a bit of truth to that comment. But how can we get a grip when it feels like things are slipping out of our control?

Anxiety is the feeling of being out of control. Whatever the issue may be, our anxiety is the signal that we cannot control what is happening. Claustrophobia is fear of small spaces—the fear being of being trapped, unable to be free. Put another way, it's fear of not being in control of your environment. Agoraphobia is the fear of entering a crowd—not being in control of who or what you might encounter. Sometimes anxiety has been part of our life for so long that we cannot identify its origin, and that really causes more anxiety.

Wherever your anxiety may originate, whatever way it plays out in your life, it is important to know the truth that God's got a grip on you. As you seek help to determine what can provide relief for your anxiety, you can know God will help you. When you talk with a counselor and create a plan, God is there with you. If along with therapy, medicine is needed to help your mind and body heal, God is with you. This truth will provide peace: you can be sure God is always with you!

A Rule of Life, very simply, is an intentional, conscious plan to keep God at the center of everything we do. It provides guidelines to help us continually remember God as the Source of our lives.

Peter Scazzero

God knows best. We can trust Him with our lives as well as our eternal souls. He does not take something from us without filling that spot with something just as good—and because it's from Him, even much better.

Janette Oke

As Luther taught, suffering is unbearable if you aren't certain that God is for you and with you.

Timothy Keller

### FOR FURTHER REFLECTION

Proverbs 3:5-6; Romans 8:28; Jeremiah 17:7

## TODAY'S PRAYER

Thank you, God, for your care for me. I pray that you will calm my fears and anxieties and help me to trust you with all of my life. Amen.

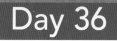

# Gifts from God

*There is nothing better than to be happy and enjoy
ourselves as long as we can. And people should eat
and drink and enjoy the fruits of their labor,
for these are gifts from God.*

ECCLESIASTES 3:12-13

We look forward to celebrations—birthdays,
weddings, graduation, and reunions, to
name a few. The joy of joining together on
milestone occasions is like the highlight reel of our life.
Remembering the look on the faces of those we love, and
how memories were being made, is such a treasure!

There are other days in which we feel the strain of
work, the shock of unwelcome news, and the isolation
of disconnection. Days like that can bring fear of the
unknown, concern and worry over how to deal with
challenges, and a feeling that God has left you in the dust.
When a number of these days get strung together it can
feel like the parts of a movie that should have been left on
the editing room floor.

Each day is a gift from God, with its beauty as well as
its tasks and challenges. Each trip around the sun offers
promise. Life is precious, but we take it for granted most
days—assuming that the day ahead will be just like all the
others before. While that is true to some extent, and some
days are better than others, we are given the gift of today!
Open each day like a gift to see what's inside and trust
that God will provide what you need.

Relying on God has to begin all over again every day as if nothing had yet been done.

C. S. Lewis

This is our time on the history line of God. This is it. What will we do with the one deep exhale of God on this earth? For we are but a vapor and we have to make it count. We're on. Direct us, Lord, and get us on our feet.

Beth Moore

What gives me the most hope every day is God's grace; knowing that his grace is going to give me the strength for whatever I face, knowing that nothing is a surprise to God.

Rick Warren

## FOR FURTHER REFLECTION

Hebrews 11; Job 11:13-19; Jeremiah 17:7-8

### TODAY'S PRAYER

Thank you, Lord, for this day. Help me celebrate today's blessings and trust you with the challenges, knowing you are with me each minute. May my life bring you glory. Amen.

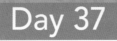

# Forever Yours

*The love of the LORD remains forever with those
who fear him. His salvation extends to
the children's children.*

PSALM 103:17

"Worst-case scenarios" are situations we imagine in which everything goes wrong. We question if we turned off the stove, or unplugged the iron, and we might even go back and check a few times. We make sure our plans are perfect and foolproof. Yet we cannot control the unknown. We will overlook a detail or just be unaware of the trouble that arises in our life and experience disappointment.

Does it seem like you'd experience less fear and anxiety if you knew everything that is going to happen in your life? Maybe not. In God's grace and mercy, we see things of this life with limited vision. God has provided his Word, his Son, and his faithful followers who help us navigate the unknown parts of life. God's faithfulness to us is the greatest strength we have no matter what we face. And as we walk with him, others will see and know that God is faithful!

The promises of God are written throughout the pages of scripture. Some are stated outright; others are told in the stories of the people in their journey of faith. The faithfulness of God is present in each promise. So is the love he has for us. We need to remind ourselves daily of these promises and rest in his unchanging way.

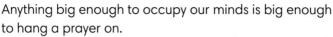

Anything big enough to occupy our minds is big enough to hang a prayer on.

George MacDonald

No challenge can stop you if you have the courage to keep moving forward in the face of your greatest fears and biggest challenges. Be courageous.

Jon Gordon

Strength of my heart, I need not fail, Not mine to fear but to obey, With such a Leader, who could quail? Thou art as Thou wert yesterday. Strength of my heart, I rest in Thee, Fulfill Thy purposes through me.

Amy Carmichael

## FOR FURTHER REFLECTION

Psalm 56:3-4; Hebrews 13:5-6; 1 Chronicles 28

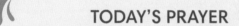

### TODAY'S PRAYER

Lord, thank you for your faithfulness to me each day. Help me to know you are at work in my life. I trust that you will fulfill your purposes for my life. Amen.

# You Are Precious

*"What is the price of two sparrows—one copper coin?*
*But not a single sparrow can fall to the ground*
*without your Father knowing it. And the very hairs*
*on your head are all numbered. So don't be afraid;*
*you are more valuable to God than a whole*
*flock of sparrows."*

MATTHEW 10:29-31

Depending on what you have experienced in your life, you may not realize your worth. Many things affect our sense of self-worth, such as parenting, experiences in childhood and beyond, and our thoughts about ourselves in relation to others. We can lose sight of the incredible truth of our value to God: You are loved and were created by God! His purpose for your life is precious and irreplaceable.

Our low self-worth can create anxiety when we are in relationships, causing us to disconnect when we feel we don't measure up. We are afraid of being rejected, so we keep our distance and isolate ourselves. Yet we were created for relationship! God knows you, created you, and loves you—and wants you to know that truth to the core of your being.

Jesus spoke the words at the top of the page to his disciples as he was preparing them to go out in ministry. These are words he is speaking to you today. He wants you to know you are precious, created in love for God's glory! Begin to recognize your value and you will begin to see the truth of who you are.

Becoming the beloved is pulling the truth revealed to me from above down into the ordinariness of what I am, in fact, thinking of, talking about and doing from hour to hour.

Henri Nouwen

My trust in God flows out of the experience of his loving me, day in and day out, whether the day is stormy or fair, whether I'm sick or in good health, whether I'm in a state of grace or disgrace. He comes to me where I live and loves me as I am.

Brennan Manning

## FOR FURTHER REFLECTION

Psalm 8:3-6; 1 John 3:1-3; Ephesians 2:10

## TODAY'S PRAYER

Heavenly Father, thank you for your love and care for me! Help me to recognize my value and worth. May this truth bring me peace and security to do your will. Amen.

# Day 39

## Sleep Well!

*Fix your thoughts on what is true, and honorable,
and right, and pure, and lovely, and admirable.
Think about things that are excellent and worthy of
praise. Keep putting into practice all you learned and
received from me—everything you heard from me and
saw me doing. Then the God of peace will be with you.*

PHILIPPIANS 4:8-9

Have you ever woken up in the night and immediately started thinking about all the things you have to do, or should not have done, or things that break your heart? It's like a switch gets flipped! Your mind swirls as you try to process all the things that pop into your mind. It's amazing that our brains can store so much information, but why does it all have to bubble up while we are trying to sleep?

Anxiety is the most common cause of plunging into troubling thoughts in the middle of the night . There are lots of strategies for getting back to sleep, and you may have tried some—pray, get out of bed, take medicine, write down your thoughts, count sheep. When we're thinking about upsetting things, it can seem impossible to focus, but it is the very best thing we can do to begin to calm our mind and get some rest.

So many times, we just allow anything into our minds. We need to be selective. The passage above is a great framework to focus your thoughts on. It is a very specific and positive list: true, honorable, right, pure, lovely, admirable, excellent and worthy of praise. Think of things that apply to each of these words. You can do this in your waking hours, too!

If you still find that you cannot get good sleep, please seek help. Sleep is so important for your brain and will help reduce anxiety in your waking hours.

God is mighty. God is caring. God is worthy of praise. God is loving. God is able. God is in control. Nothing takes God by surprise. Some sweet truths to hold onto tonight.

Lysa TerKeurst

Courage, then, and patience! Courage for the great sorrows of life, and patience for the small ones. And then when you have laboriously accomplished your daily task, go to sleep in peace. God is awake.

Victor Hugo

## FOR FURTHER REFLECTION

Psalm 91:9-11; John 14:27; Psalm 121

### TODAY'S PRAYER

Lord God, help me to recall the blessings in my life as I go throughout my day. Please bless me with good sleep, comforted by knowing you are sovereign. Amen.

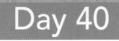

# Thinking Patterns

*Hold on to the pattern of wholesome teaching you learned from me—a pattern shaped by the faith and love that you have in Christ Jesus. Through the power of the Holy Spirit who lives within us, carefully guard the precious truth that has been entrusted to you.*

2 TIMOTHY 1:13-14

We are all creatures of habit,—not only bad habits, but routines and patterns in our daily lives which help shape our character. Anxiety and fear can become a habit. That sounds weird; who would want to routinely feel anxious or afraid? Yet many of us live in a pattern of fear and anxiety and think there is no way to change it. But there is. .

Think about times when you were not feeling anxious or fearful. What was happening? Were you celebrating? Were you engrossed in a good book or movie, or learning something new? Were you with a good friend? To change our thinking patterns, we have to disrupt that which our minds routinely swirl around. Start small, and you will begin to develop routines that are healthy. It could be exercise; your brain benefits from the chemicals that are released through physical activity. Maybe take up a hobby, join a Bible study, or learn to meditate on the scriptures. The idea is to develop and solidify new patterns. But don't try to change them all at one time—it won't work, and you will be stressed!

The patterns of our lives are ours to change. In 12-step recovery, people learn new ways of thinking, because to regain their lives they need to change their routines and mindsets. As you change the patterns in your life, you will begin to experience peace of mind and clarity, which become the new patterns.

We can't solve problems by using the same kind of thinking we used when we created them.

Albert Einstein

If you feel stuck, bring your whole self to Christ, not just the problem, but you. Ask God to change your heart. Commit yourself to pray to that end. It's God's heart to give good gifts to His children.

Sheila Walsh

## FOR FURTHER REFLECTION

Romans 12:1-2; Proverbs 3:1-8;
2 Corinthians 5:14-17

### TODAY'S PRAYER

Lord, help me to discern the patterns of my thinking. Help me become the person you have created me to be and to experience freedom from fear and anxiety. Amen.

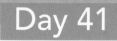
# God Loves You!

*How precious are your thoughts about me, O God.*
*They cannot be numbered! I can't even count them;*
*they outnumber the grains of sand! And when*
*I wake up, you are still with me!*

PSALM 139:17-18

D o you ever wonder how God thinks about you?
Our understanding of what God thinks about us
is shaped by many different messages we pick up
throughout our lives. Our earthly father has a big impact
on our perceptions of our heavenly father, and across our
lifetimes we also hear other influential voices tell us what
they think about us, good or bad. We need to measure
those messages against what God says about us.

When we feel insecure about who we are, fear is a
common outcome. Our anxiety builds as we doubt our
value or worth—in our work, our relationships, and the
world we live in. Fear causes us to feel alone, on our own
to handle whatever may be challenging us in our lives.
Even followers of Christ may lose sight of the strength
of our faith. We wonder, "Where is God?" In the scariest
situations we may not realize he never left. He is with us
in the midst of it all.

The truth is, God's opinion of you is that you are
precious, loved, you are worthy, you have value, and you
were created with a purpose. Spend time in God's Word
to discover what he says about you and begin to know
without a doubt!

Whatever I may know about God, I won't really know God personally until I spend time with Him and depend on Him.

Renee Swope

The vehicle for gaining intimacy with God as a Christian is regular communication with God. We are to listen to God as he speaks to us through his Word, and we are to respond to God with our honest thoughts, feelings, and decisions.

Gary Chapman

Love will never condemn you for being lost, but love will not let you stay there alone, even though it will never force you to come out of your hiding places.

Wm. Paul Young

## FOR FURTHER REFLECTION

1 John 3:1-3; Jeremiah 29:11-13; John 3:16

### TODAY'S PRAYER

Thank you, God, for loving me and for your loving kindness towards me. Help me to see myself through the way you do, and fulfill the purpose you have for my life. Amen.

# Grace

*He said, "My grace is all you need. My power works best in weakness." So now I am glad to boast about my weaknesses, so that the power of Christ can work through me.*

2 Corinthians 12:9

Grace, in the biblical definition, is the unmerited favor of God, the free gift of salvation. It is hard for us to describe, but we are so grateful when we receive this powerful gift in our lives. How does grace affect our fears and anxiety? It can provide relief as we trust that God is going to work things out according to his will and purpose.

This passage says that Christ's power works best in our weakness. Our fears and anxieties can make us feel unable to handle whatever is in front of us. We try to be courageous, but at times we feel stuck in our fear and anxiety. In those moments we can look to the Lord and surrender ourselves to him, knowing he will provide. Grace upon grace, God empowers us to move forward on our journey.

Where do you need God's grace today? Is there something that you are finding it difficult to handle in your own strength? Offer it to Jesus today and begin to experience his grace, which is always enough for the day!

Without a heart transformed by the grace of Christ, we just continue to manage external and internal darkness.

Matt Chandler

But grace does more. It connects us to the invisible One in an eternal love relationship that fills us with joy we have never known before and gives us rest of heart that we would have thought impossible. And that grace is still rescuing us, because we still tend to forget what is important, real, and true.

Paul David Tripp

Grace is God's best idea. His decision to ravage a people by love, to rescue passionately, and to restore justly—what rivals it? Of all his wondrous works, grace, in my estimation, is the magnum opus.

Max Lucado

## For further reflection

2 Timothy 1:9; John 1:16-17; Hebrews 4:14-16

### TODAY'S PRAYER

Dear Jesus, thank you for your abundant grace! Help me to recognize your grace is at work and surrender to you to experience your peace. Amen.

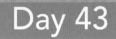

# Day 43

## Seek and Find

*Trust in the LORD with all your heart; do not depend on your own understanding. Seek his will in all you do, and he will show you which path to take.*

PROVERBS 3:5-6

Struggling with fear and anxiety is very closely related to not knowing what is happening. If we knew more, we could relax, right? Maybe not! Think about some of the challenges you have faced— would you have felt better if you'd known ahead of time what would happen? It really is hard to discern which things you need to know, and which ones are better left unknown until they happen.

Building our trust in God's ability to care, guide, and provide for us is a daily process. God is trustworthy and faithful, and he loves us completely. We learn to trust him through learning about who God is, what he thinks of us, and how he has worked in our lives. Then in times of trial we will seek him and find him.

God created you with a purpose. He knows you completely! When you are anxious and fearful about something, the best path forward is to trust God's wisdom and providence. Life will always have uncertainties, but we serve a God who is sovereign and faithful!

Faith isn't the ability to believe long and far into the misty future. It's simply taking God at His Word and taking the next step.

Joni Eareckson Tada

We must cease striving and trust God to provide what He thinks is best and in whatever time He chooses to make it available. But this kind of trusting doesn't come naturally. It's a spiritual crisis of the will in which we must choose to exercise faith.

Chuck Swindoll

If you are caught up in situations beyond your control, the solution is not figuring out how God can save you; it's trusting that he will.

Linda Evans Shepherd

## FOR FURTHER REFLECTION

Lamentations 3:22-23; Philippians 4:5-6;
Romans 12:12

### TODAY'S PRAYER

Lord, help me trust you each day with every part of my life. I know you will lead me on the best path for my life. Thank you for your ever-present help and guidance. Amen.

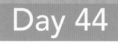

# Gratitude Mindset

*Give thanks to the Lord, for he is good!*
*His faithful love endures forever.*

Psalm 136:1

We are created with powerful minds! Imagine all of the things that have been discovered, created, and developed through the great minds of mere humans! But powerful imaginations also can create really bad things that breed fear, worry, and distrust. The world is full of things that are not beneficial for our hearts and minds. When we are overexposed to negativity, we begin to feel the effects in ways we may not realize.

You cannot live in a bubble where nothing goes wrong, but you can choose what you expose yourself to on a regular basis. If you want to experience peace and calm, watching a scary movie or reading a murder mystery novel probably isn't the best choice. Instead, you might want to watch something that isn't designed to make you jump out of your seat. Being selective about what you take into your mind can create peace and a calm mind.

When our fears and anxieties threaten to occupy our minds, gratitude is a great way to fill it with the opposite thoughts. Psalm 136 is a list of the blessings that the writer is focusing on, along with the refrain "His faithful love endures forever." God is faithful! He will provide for our needs! This is something we can be grateful for!

Meditate—fill your mind—with the words of this psalm and begin to discover the power of a calm, peaceful mind.

Nothing done with the focus on God is ever a waste of time.

Lysa TerKeurst

I want to take my focus off myself and focus on God. It's like setting your spiritual compass so no matter which way you turn during the day, whatever comes up, then my thoughts go back to Him and whatever He said that morning.

Anne Graham Lotz

When we have God in clear focus, His powerful presence eclipses our fears.

Chuck Swindoll

## FOR FURTHER REFLECTION

Isaiah 35; Philippians 4:10-14; Galatians 5:22-26

### TODAY'S PRAYER

Lord, I am so grateful for your presence in my life! Help me as I make choices about what I allow to fill my thoughts. You are worthy of praise! Amen.

# Perfect Peace

*You will keep in perfect peace all who trust in you,*
*all whose thoughts are fixed on you!*

ISAIAH 26:3

Perfectionism is a state of mind that is constantly in motion, always trying to find the "perfect" in every situation. Initially, that doesn't sound like a bad thing; we want to do our best in everything, and so we seek to improve whatever we can. Sometimes, though, this goal becomes the focus of our thoughts. As we chase after the elusive "perfect," we are not at peace, because something always needs to be improved.

The passage above claims that God will give "perfect peace" to all who trust in him. Philippians 4:7 speaks of "peace that exceeds anything we can understand. " That is the type of peace God promises to you as you fix your thoughts on God.

What does it mean to "fix your thoughts on God"? It means that in every situation you are seeking God's way—not what the world describes as "perfect" (which falls far short of God's standard) or what you, in your own thoughts, decide is perfect. In times when you are unsure of what is best, begin to ask God. Trust in his timing and his way and you will begin to experience perfect peace.

Real contentment must come from within. You and I cannot change or control the world around us, but we can change and control the world within us.

Warren Wiersbe

The labor of self-love is a heavy one indeed. Think whether much of your sorrow has not arisen from someone speaking slightingly of you. As long as you set yourself up as a little god to which you must be loyal there will be those who will delight to offer affront to your idol. How then can you hope to have inward peace?

A. W. Tozer

Blessed are the single-hearted, for they shall enjoy much peace. . . . If you refuse to be hurried and pressed, if you stay your soul on God, nothing can keep you from that clearness of spirit which is life and peace. . . . In that stillness you know what His will is.

Amy Carmichael

## For further reflection

Philippians 4:6-9; John 16:31-33; Psalm 4:6-8

## TODAY'S PRAYER

Lord, fill me with your peace. Help me to know your way for my life. Help me rest in you alone and experience your perfect peace. Amen.

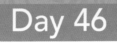

# Day 46

## Powerful God!

*God is our refuge and strength, always ready*
*to help in times of trouble.*

<small>PSALM 46:1</small>

Anxieties and fears weaken our resolve, create uncertainty, and make us feel like we are alone in our struggles. Our worries can make us feel incompetent and confused, and we get stuck. As we try to power alone through the challenges in our lives, we resist the strength that God provides. How's that working for you?

You may have experienced disappointment with God—prayers that weren't answered the way you wanted, or deep losses that you blame God for allowing to happen. Disappointment can interrupt the truth that God is powerful and able to help us in our time of need. How can we increase our belief in the truth that God is our help and refuge in times of trouble?

Changing your view of God is integral to experiencing his strength and peace. We need to grasp that life will not always turn out the way we had hoped, but God will make a way in the difficulty. The great challenges we experience will not go unnoticed by our Heavenly Father—he will see us through. Resist the lie that you are on your own in life. Ask for help and strength each day from the One who created everything. He is able!

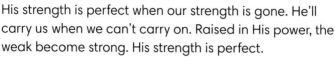

His strength is perfect when our strength is gone. He'll carry us when we can't carry on. Raised in His power, the weak become strong. His strength is perfect.

Jerry Salley and Steven Curtis Chapman

Remember, it is not your weakness that will get in the way of God's working through you, but your delusions of strength. His strength is made perfect in our weakness! Point to His strength by being willing to admit your weakness.

Paul David Tripp

We serve a God who says that even when we're under pressure and feel like nothing is going to go right, he is waiting for us, to embrace us whether we succeed or fail.

Max Lucado

## FOR FURTHER REFLECTION

Deuteronomy 31:6-8; Psalm 28:7; Ephesians 6:10-18

### TODAY'S PRAYER

Dear God, help me recognize that you are with me in every situation, every moment, and you will provide everything I need. Thank you for your power at work in my life! Amen.

# Day 47

## New Strength

*Those who trust in the LORD will find new strength.*
*They will soar high on wings like eagles. They will*
*run and not grow weary. They will walk and not faint.*

ISAIAH 40:31

Are you worn out from the struggles you are worried about? Fearful of what is going to happen next? Life can be so exhausting—especially on days that seem to blend one into the ones before, so that you lose track of time. If you have been walking through a desperate situation where hope seems to be lost, you can feel like you have no strength to continue.

Today, believe that no matter what is weighing you down, God will lift you up. Nothing is too hard for the Lord. You are not the exception to his mighty power. Your situation is not a surprise to him, and God will provide his strength for each step and a new spirit of encouragement and energy to face the day. You can trust your concerns and fears to God. Experience the strength God offers you as you trust him with all of your life.

Trust in the Lord! He will provide new strength to help you continue on the journey! What a promise! Through difficulties, sorrows, and times when you feel disconnected, the Lord will provide new strength.

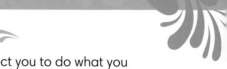

A faithful God does not expect you to do what you cannot; He supplies the needed strength.

Erwin Lutzer

We can't anticipate and provide for life's trials, but the Lord can and does. The Lord wants us to thirst not after a quick fix to our problems but after the life-altering refreshment of His provision.

Priscilla Shirer

God does not give us everything we want, but He does fulfill all His promises . . . leading us along the best and straightest paths to Himself.

Dietrich Bonhoeffer

## FOR FURTHER REFLECTION

Matthew 6:32-34; Psalm 62; 2 Corinthians 12:9-10

### TODAY'S PRAYER

Lord, I need your strength for this day and every day. As I ask for your help, help me to receive all that you have for me. Thank you for your loving care for me. Amen.

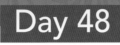

# Day 48

## Fail-Safe

*The word of God will never fail.*

LUKE 1:37

When we experience losses, unexpected challenges, or overwhelming circumstances, we begin to look for ways to live a fail-safe life. We want a life in which nothing bad will happen, so we can feel secure. Good luck with that plan. Life just doesn't work that way.

Fail-safe describes the safety net that is built in so that if something bad happens, there is another way to prevent disaster. Wouldn't it be great for our lives to be fail-safe? As we go on high alert looking for help, resources, and safety, we can develop the illusion that we are prepared for the worst possible situation. We may be ready for action, but our lives still are not fail-safe.

Because we are human, we know that nothing in this world is fail-safe. We ultimately will face uncertainty and challenges in our lives. Yet, in the midst of this, God's Word never fails! It truly is the only fail-safe thing in our lives. When you know that God loves you, has a plan for your life, and provides a way of redemption, you can rest in this truth. As you read God's Word and meditate on the scripture, you will begin to know what God is saying to you and about the reality of life. No matter what you face you will know God's way through his Word. You will begin to trust God more and more!

God is God. Because He is God, He is worthy of my trust and obedience. I will find rest nowhere but in His holy will, a will that is unspeakably beyond my largest notions of what He is up to.

Elisabeth Elliot

Having your spiritual radar up in constant anticipation of His presence—even in the midst of the joyful chaos and regular rhythms of your everyday living—is paramount in hearing God, because sometimes the place and manner you find Him is the least spectacular you'd expect.

Priscilla Shirer

Faith is taking one step when it's only one step you see simply because you believe God wants you to do it based on His Word. It is taking a step without being assured of the destination.

Tony Evans

## FOR FURTHER REFLECTION

Proverbs 3:5-6; Philippians 4:6-7;
Lamentations 3:22-23

### TODAY'S PRAYER

Heavenly Father, thank you for your faithfulness! Your Word brings truth to my life and I know it is trustworthy. You are an awesome God! Amen.

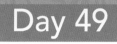

# Day 49

## Equipped

*Put on every piece of God's armor so you will be able to resist the enemy in the time of evil. Then after the battle you will still be standing firm.*

EPHESIANS 6:13

D o you ever feel ill equipped for your life? Like you have a pop quiz every day and you have no idea what will be on it? That is how anxiety can make you feel—like you are supposed to know everything the minute you are asked a question or faced with a decision. It makes every decision seem loaded, as though one wrong answer will start a domino effect and the rest of your life will tumble down. You feel shame—because aren't you old enough or smart enough to figure things out?

We all want to know exactly what to say, when to say it, and how to make good decisions for our lives. But anxiety can keep us from learning new ways to deal with things. It can hold us back from asking questions to discover new information that could help us make good decisions. There's an acrostic for shame—Should Have Already Mastered Everything. When we feel unprepared, when we feel we don't measure up to others, when we feel like we should already know things we do not, anxiety can make us resist asking for help. Instead, we isolate.

To heal the shame, begin to recognize it is not from God. He loves you and has redeemed your life. In his timing, the Lord will provide the answers you need. Until then you can rest, knowing you aren't in charge of everything.

Nobody knows everything, and we don't need to feel ashamed about it. Preparing for life's pop quizzes requires a heart surrendered to Christ, and daily connection through the Bible and prayer that releases your desires, concerns, and needs. Then you will be equipped for whatever may come across your path.

Empathy's the antidote to shame. The two most powerful words when we're in struggle: me too.

Brené Brown

May God remind us daily—no matter what kind of obstacles we face—that we are loved and empowered by the One who brought the universe into existence with the mere sound of His voice. Nothing is impossible for Him.

Beth Moore

If guilt tells us that we've done something wrong, then shame tells us that we are something wrong. So many people feel isolated, not good enough, defined by the labels they wear rather than the identity they have in Christ.

Sheila Walsh

## For further reflection

Isaiah 61:7; Psalm 34:4-5; Isaiah 50:7-10

### TODAY'S PRAYER

Lord, help me trust you with the answers to all the questions I face. I am thankful that you know me, love me, and will be with me as I journey through life. Amen.

# Comfort

*May our Lord Jesus Christ himself and God our
Father, who loved us and by his grace gave us eternal
comfort and a wonderful hope, comfort you and
strengthen you in every good thing you do and say.*

2 THESSALONIANS 2:16-17

Do you need a hug? Would you like someone to provide support and a listening ear, a calming presence, and reassurance that it will all work out? Sometimes the answer is "Yes, actually that would be helpful." Other times it feels like nothing will help.

The comfort of Christ isn't like some sentiment in a greeting card. It is the foundation you can build your life upon. Knowing that you are loved and cared for by the Son of God is no small thing. This love and care often come through the body of Christ—believers who are the hands and feet of Jesus, who offer support and comfort in our time of need. Connection is so much a part of our healing process!

When we are concerned and fearful, we can isolate ourselves from the people who are asking what they can do to help. It can feel invasive, overwhelming, and our anxiety can cause us to reject their offers of comfort and care. You wouldn't reject Jesus if he asked you, "What's wrong? How can I help?" Allow yourself to receive the love and care of Christ through his body of believers. If in the past you have rejected other people's attempts to support you, maybe it's time to reach out to those who offered and ask for help. We all struggle, and we can all help each other in tough times.

Snuggle in God's arms. When you are hurting, when you feel lonely, left out, let Him cradle you, comfort you, reassure you of His all-sufficient power and love.

Kay Arthur

We're often ashamed of asking for so much help because it seems selfish or petty or narcissistic, but I think, if there's a God—and I believe there is—that God is there to help. That's what God's job is.

Anne Lamott

Christian life isn't a one-person race. It's a relay. You are not alone; you're part of a team assembled by our unstoppable God to achieve his eternal purposes.

Christine Caine

## For further reflection

Psalm 23; Romans 8:37-39; Isaiah 49:13

## TODAY'S PRAYER

Jesus, be near to me today, through the body of believers. Thank you for your love and care for me through your people. Amen.

# Faithful

*The faithful love of the LORD never ends!*
*His mercies never cease. Great is his faithfulness;*
*his mercies begin afresh each morning.*

<small>LAMENTATIONS 3:22-23</small>

When fear and anxiety rule our lives, we can feel as though we are on our own to deal with the unknown. This is sometimes referred to as "the dark night of the soul." We are stretched to our emotional limits, and maybe close to the edge in terms of practical resources. We are losing hope. We can spiral down so far into our anxious thoughts that we lose sight of the truth that God is faithful.

Fear and anxiety create a barrier between us and the truth. We begin to believe lies like, "It's over," "It will never get better," or "I will never get through this." Yet the story isn't over. The worst thing that can happen in our lives is not a surprise to God. He is present in the very pit and is there to provide a way out—in his time.

Chapter 3 of Lamentations describes the writer's experience of being in a pit. As you read through the verses you may agree with them! The turning point is in verse 21: "Yet I still dare to hope." In your distress, will you dare to hope? God is faithful and provides grace and mercy for you today!

God is the only one who can make the valley of trouble a door of hope.

Catherine Marshall

It's always something, to know you've done the most you could. But, don't leave off hoping, or it's of no use doing anything. Hope, hope to the last.

Charles Dickens, *Nicholas Nickleby*

If God can bring blessing from the broken body of Jesus and glory from something that's as obscene as the cross, He can bring blessing from my problems and my pain and my unanswered prayer. I just have to trust Him.

Anne Graham Lotz

## FOR FURTHER REFLECTION

Romans 15:13; Deuteronomy 31:6; Micah 7:7

### TODAY'S PRAYER

Heavenly Father, you are a faithful God. Help me to trust you with all that I am holding onto. Help me to rest in the truth that you are able to provide a hope and a future for me. Amen.

# Waiting Well

*I wait quietly before God, for my victory comes from him. He alone is my rock and my salvation, my fortress where I will never be shaken.*

PSALM 62:1-2

Waiting well requires patience and endurance, for we don't know when the answer or resolution will come. You can work yourself up with worry and fear that the result will not be what you had hoped. Thinking of all the options and endings, sometimes the worst possible scenario is all you can focus on.

In times like these what you need is a stable foundation on which to stand. While you wait, focus on the truth that God is working on your problem or situation. No matter what the outcome, God will provide strength for you. Waiting well requires stability, a core of peace that will pervade every part of your thoughts. Accepting that God is trustworthy, strong, and faithful will calm and quiet your mind. When the temptation to panic arises, choose to focus on the fortress that God provides for you. Trust that he is going before you and will provide wisdom and insight—and rest on these promises.

If you are in a season of waiting, choose to wait well—resting in the strength of the Lord, knowing he will give you a solid place on which to wait. Ask God for peace as you choose to wait well.

If any are inclined to despond, because they have not such patience, let them be of good courage; it is in the course of our feeble and very imperfect waiting that God Himself, by His hidden power, strengthens us and works out in us the patience of the great saints, the patience of Christ Himself.

Andrew Murray

Teach us, O Lord, the disciplines of patience, for to wait is often harder than to work.

Peter Marshall

I don't have to figure my present circumstances out. I don't have to fill the silence left behind in another person's absence. I don't have to know all the whys and what-ifs. All I have to do is trust. So, in quiet humility and without personal agenda, I make the decision to let God sort it all out. I sit quietly in His presence and simply say, "God, I want Your truth to be the loudest voice in my life. Correct me. Comfort me. Come closer still. And I will trust. God, You are good at being God."

Lysa TerKeurst

## FOR FURTHER REFLECTION

2 Corinthians 4:16-18; Psalm 130:5-6;
Isaiah 40:30-33

### TODAY'S PRAYER

Lord God, you are my rock and fortress! Help me to seek your peace as I wait on you to work in my life, trusting that no matter what I face you will always be my shelter. Amen.

# Self-Awareness

*See how very much our Father loves us, for he calls us his children, and that is what we are! But the people who belong to this world don't recognize that we are God's children because they don't know him.*

1 JOHN 3:1

Do you know who you are? You might wonder what this question has to do with anxiety or fear. Our identities are core to the way we experience the world around us. When we are unsure of who we are and who loves us, we feel disconnected, which creates anxiety and fear. Our upbringing, self-defeating thoughts, and trauma all have an impact on our identity. We may be living with a distorted sense of who we really are.

Being unsure of what others think of us, or unsure of our environment, can sometimes cause us to be reactive. Self-awareness—knowing who you are, and your value—can provide a sense of security and serenity. Recognizing that our Heavenly Father calls us his very own children is a great foundation for our identity. God loves you, and that truth can change the very way you experience life.

If you are not sure that you are valuable to God, if you aren't confident of how very much he loves you, decide to take this truth to heart. Experience the joy that comes when you know beyond any doubt that God calls you his child! Shame will be replaced by love. You will experience peace and joy as you become aware of whose you are.

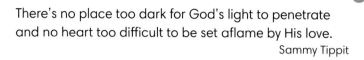

There's no place too dark for God's light to penetrate and no heart too difficult to be set aflame by His love.

Sammy Tippit

The greatest honor we can give Almighty God is to live gladly because of the knowledge of his love.

Julian of Norwich

We're going to have to let truth scream louder to our souls than the lies that have infected us.

Beth Moore

## For further reflection

Ephesians 2:4-5; John 3:16-18; Zephaniah 3:17

### TODAY'S PRAYER

Thank you, Lord, for loving me! Help me to know this truth to my core and to live in your love each minute. Amen.

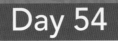
# Fruitful Life

*The Holy Spirit produces this kind of fruit in our
lives: love, joy, peace, patience, kindness, goodness,
faithfulness, gentleness, and self-control.
There is no law against these things!*

GALATIANS 5:22-23

As followers of Christ, we are given the gift of the Holy Spirit. The Holy Spirit helps us as we grow in our awareness of how to live our lives centered on Jesus and his teachings. The challenge is that we are human, living our physical life on earth. It takes supernatural power to change us to be more and more like Jesus. That is why the Holy Spirit was given to us!

Anxiety and fear are very much a part of the human condition. For some of us they are so powerful that we are not experiencing the fruit of the Holy Spirit; love, joy, peace, patience, kindness, goodness, faithfulness, gentleness and self-control. It's not because we don't want to; it's just that our fears and anxieties can challenge the growth of this fruit. Don't be discouraged— there is hope!

The Holy Spirit works through prayer, God's Word, counseling, and support through other people. As healing begins, you will feel more of each of these fruits and know that the Spirit is working in your life. As you continue to seek God's wisdom and truth for your life, you will grow and experience freedom in Christ.

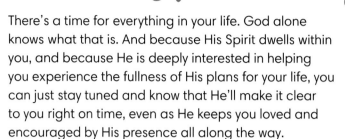

There's a time for everything in your life. God alone knows what that is. And because His Spirit dwells within you, and because He is deeply interested in helping you experience the fullness of His plans for your life, you can just stay tuned and know that He'll make it clear to you right on time, even as He keeps you loved and encouraged by His presence all along the way.

Priscilla Shirer

The Spirit-filled life is not a special, deluxe edition of Christianity. It is part and parcel of the total plan of God for His people.

A. W. Tozer

I believe God, through His Spirit, grants us love, joy, and peace no matter what is happening in our lives. As Christians, we shouldn't expect our joy to always feel like happiness, but instead recognize joy as inner security—a safeness in our life with Christ.

Jill Briscoe

## For further reflection

Romans 8:2-6; 2 Corinthians 3:16-18; 1 John 2:19-27

### TODAY'S PRAYER

Thank you, Jesus, for your gift of the Holy Spirit! Help me to be aware of the way you are guiding my life through this gift! Thank you for your presence. Amen.

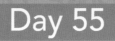

# Day 55

## The Blessing

*May the LORD bless you and protect you. May the
LORD smile on you and be gracious to you. May the
LORD show you his favor and give you his peace.*

NUMBERS 6:24-26

When you feel troubled and apprehensive, do you long for reassurance that God is with you? Feeling alone in your struggles can intensify that feeling. The presence of God is sometimes difficult to perceive when other feelings overwhelm our thoughts. Our concerns and cares tend to become the only presence we sense, and they consume our days and nights. The truth is that God is always with you. The challenge is for you to be aware of this truth.

Anxious thoughts are like the "spinning wheel of death" when your device is searching for connection—they spin and spin the worries and cares we carry, preventing connection and rest we need. Apprehension sets in as "'what ifs" pervade our minds. At such times it is imperative to seek the Lord and pray for a sense of his presence and peace. God is always with you, even though you may be walking through a difficult season or if it feels like your whole life has been challenging, God loves you and cares for you.

In the book of Numbers, God instructs Moses to have Aaron bless the Israelites with the words at the top of this page. They are a beautiful reminder of the blessing of God's presence. These ancient words still hold truth and meaning for your life today. Despite the challenges of life, we can experience the blessing of God each and every day! Commit this passage to memory and repeat it often as a reminder of the blessing of the Lord on your life.

An infinite God can give all of Himself to each of His children. He does not distribute Himself that each may have a part, but to each one He gives all of Himself as fully as if there were no others.

A. W. Tozer

We like to control the map of our life and know everything well in advance. But faith is content just knowing that God's promise cannot fail. This, in fact, is the excitement of walking with God.

Jim Cymbala

In your brokenness & imperfection, God whispers three words: You are mine.

Margaret Feinberg

## FOR FURTHER REFLECTION

Isaiah 41:10-12; Psalm 34:17-18; Psalm 145:13-21

## TODAY'S PRAYER

Thank you, Lord for your presence in my life! Strengthen and comfort me with the knowledge that you are always with me. I receive your blessing as a precious gift to be opened each morning. Amen.

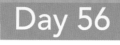

# Day 56

## Need to Know

*For the LORD grants wisdom! From his mouth*
*come knowledge and understanding.*

PROVERBS 2:6

Concerns and challenges do not come with a set of instructions about how to fix them. Wouldn't that help? Just knowing what to do next would provide peace and assurance that would help us move forward to resolve the issues. Unfortunately, this isn't the way it works.

Think about a pressing problem you are experiencing today. You may have made a list of what needs to happen, you may have consulted with trusted friends and advisors, and yet still feel uncertain about what the next step looks like. There is nothing wrong with making lists, talking with others, and doing research as you approach a problem. However, they don't always provide understanding and clarity. You need the Lord's wisdom every day!

As you work through possible ways to resolve the issues you face, remember to pray. Ask God for wisdom, knowledge, and understanding about the problems. Ask the Lord to provide insight and a sense of peace. God will provide. We need to know how to move forward and we can trust the Lord's wisdom and understanding for any challenge we face.

A saying I heard years ago: "It doesn't matter what you do. Just do something, even if it's wrong!" That's the most stupid counsel I've ever heard. Never do what's wrong! Do nothing until it's right. Then do it with all your might. That's wise counsel.

Chuck Swindoll

Replace what you don't know about the future with what you do know about God!

Christine Caine

Authentic faith cannot help but act.

Beth Moore

## FOR FURTHER REFLECTION

Psalm 111:10; James 3:17; Colossians 2:2-3

## TODAY'S PRAYER

Dear Heavenly Father, I trust that you will provide wisdom for what I am facing. Help me as I seek your clarity and assurance about what steps to take. I recognize that your way is best. Amen.

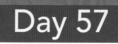

# Day 57

# Provision

*For the LORD God is our sun and our shield. He gives us grace and glory. The LORD will withhold no good thing from those who do what is right. O LORD of Heaven's Armies, what joy for those who trust in you.*

PSALM 84:11-12

What will it take for you to consider this day a "good day"? Are you feeling overwhelmed by the list of tasks you are facing? Is your heart breaking because of a loss? Are you uncertain what the future holds for you? No matter what you have on your heart today, God will provide.

What we believe about God's provision has a direct impact on our level of anxiety and fear every day. When you believe that "it's all on you," you can lose sight of the truth that God will provide just what we need, just at the time when we need it. Even on days when it feels like God's late to the game, we have to build our trust that his timing is perfect.

Whatever you are facing today—whether it feels insurmountable, or is just a small thing that is irritating you—trust that God will provide. Be reassured: God's promises are a foundation upon which you can build your life. Trusting that God will provide in every situation in your life is the pathway to joy.

God knows what each one of us is dealing with. He knows our pressures. He knows our conflicts. And He has made a provision for each and every one of them. That provision is Himself in the person of the Holy Spirit, indwelling us and empowering us to respond rightly.

Kay Arthur

We can be certain that God will give us the strength and resources we need to live through any situation in life that he ordains. The will of God will never take us where the grace of God cannot sustain us.

Billy Graham

A God wise enough to create me and the world I live in is wise enough to watch out for me.

Philip Yancey

## For further reflection

Philippians 4:18-19; Luke 12:31; Matthew 7:7

## TODAY'S PRAYER

Lord God, You are the giver of life. You have provided for me all my days, and I am grateful! Help me to rest in the truth that you will provide what I need for each day. Thank you for loving me so much! Amen.

# Inseparable!

*I am convinced that nothing can ever separate us
from God's love. Neither death nor life, neither angels
nor demons, neither our fears for today nor our
worries about tomorrow—not even the powers of hell
can separate us from God's love. No power in the sky
above or in the earth below—indeed, nothing in all
creation will ever be able to separate us from the love
of God that is revealed in Christ Jesus our Lord.*

ROMANS 8:38-39

We usually associate separation anxiety with young children who don't like being away from their parents. It typically occurs near the toddler age, and it can be pretty intense. The child has difficulty managing the big feelings of being apart from the main adults who provide love and care for them. If you have ever had a child with separation anxiety—or have felt this yourself—you know the overpowering feelings that accompany it.

As adults, we may experience anxiety as a result of feeling separated from God's love. Sometimes guilt or shame can create distance in our relationship with God—but not because of God. He loves us completely and always will! Our feelings create the distance, and can perpetuate that distance as we feel unworthy of God's love, forgiveness, and acceptance.

Are you feeling distant from God due to guilt or shame? Do you feel you are not good enough?—that somehow God couldn't love you? Reject these lies. Today, know that God loves you—completely! Nothing will separate you from

God's love! Knowing this truth will change everything for you. You will experience peace and joy as you know without a doubt that you are loved by God.

God loves each of us as if there were only one of us.

Saint Augustine

Faithfulness is that with which God meets us in secret, so on our part there should be the childlike simplicity of faith, the confidence that our prayer does bring down a blessing.

Andrew Murray

No matter who you are or what kind of baggage you carry with you, no matter what you look like or feel like, no matter what you do or don't do, God loves you just as you are right now. You don't have to get your act together, lose ten pounds, run a marathon, write a best-selling book, or raise perfect children. You are an extraordinary woman/man in His sight right now.

Beth Moore

## FOR FURTHER REFLECTION

1 John 3:1; John 15:9-13; Ephesians 2:4-5

## TODAY'S PRAYER

Thank you, Lord, for your never failing love for me! Help me to be confident of your love and to experience the peace and assurance that only your love can provide. Amen.

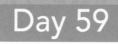
## Prayer

*As for me, I look to the LORD for help.*
*I wait confidently for God to save me,*
*and my God will certainly hear me.*

MICAH 7:7

The concerns and cares that fill your mind can cloud your thinking. "What ifs" and thoughts like "how can it be" can make us hyper-focus on a problem, and distract us from asking for help. Looking at a problem from all sides isn't necessarily wrong—but it leaves out the Lord, who can provide insight and hope for you.

Surprisingly, many believers don't always pray when they are filled with worry. They talk about praying, and they ask others to pray, but they barely spend time with God themselves asking for help in their situation. Have you prayed about your concerns as much as you have talked about them? If you are not praying for God's help and wisdom, you may be missing out on the very answer you are waiting for in your situation.

God is waiting for you, always, to share your heart, your worries, and your victories. As you spend time in prayer with God, you begin to know him more, which will increase your trust in him. You will come to know that he is always ready to listen to you and provide what you need for your life. This promise will give you hope no matter what happens.

The reality is, my prayers don't change God. But I am convinced prayer changes me. Praying boldly boots me out of that stale place of religious habit into authentic connection with God Himself.

Lysa TerKeurst

Our prayers may be awkward. Our attempts may be feeble. But since the power of prayer is in the one who hears it and not in the one who says it, our prayers do make a difference.

Max Lucado

Is prayer your steering wheel or your spare tire?

Corrie ten Boom

## FOR FURTHER REFLECTION

Matthew 6:9-13; 1 John 5:14-16; 2 Chronicles 7:14

### TODAY'S PRAYER

Lord Jesus, thank you for your listening ear. Help me as I bring my concerns, cares, and celebrations to you. I am grateful for your constant presence and assurance. Amen.

# Eternal Relief

*He will wipe every tear from their eyes, and there*
*will be no more death or sorrow or crying or pain.*
*All these things are gone forever.*

REVELATION 21:4

If you have been carrying burdens for years, your heart heavy with concerns for loved ones and worries about unresolved situations, you may feel like things will never get better. You may have had traumatic losses that have created unrelenting anxiety about your future. Our worries and fears become a way of life that seems unending.

God promises to always be with you, to bear your burdens, and to provide comfort. All you need to do is to surrender to him daily, in prayer, your burdens, cares, and concerns. That phrase "all you need to do" can feel like a ton of bricks sitting on your chest, though. It sounds simple—yet it can be so hard to even express what is on our hearts. However, if you begin by praying about just one thing that worries you, and continue with this practice, you will soon find that sharing your heart with the Lord on a daily basis brings you comfort.

We have the promise of eternal relief in the presence of God when we are with him forever in eternity. Until then, you can depend on his presence for strength and comfort as you continue on your journey here on earth. To begin to experience his relief today, pray about everything that is on your heart and mind. He will comfort you!

Whether our fear is absolutely realistic or out of proportion in our minds, our greatest refuge is Jesus Christ.

Luci Swindoll

I have held many things in my hands, and I have lost them all; but whatever I have placed in God's hands, that I still possess.

Martin Luther

The ultimate freedom we have as human beings is the power to select what we will allow or require our minds to dwell upon.

Dallas Willard

## FOR FURTHER REFLECTION

Exodus 15:2; 2 Corinthians 12:9-10;
Matthew 21:21-22

## TODAY'S PRAYER

Lord, I bring my whole heart to you today, trusting that you are with me in my struggles and that in all these things, you will provide your love and care for me. Thank you for your faithfulness and your promise of eternal hope. Amen.

## Soulful Rest

*Then Jesus said, "Come to me, all of you who are
weary and carry heavy burdens, and I will give you
rest. Take my yoke upon you. Let me teach you,
because I am humble and gentle at heart, and you
will find rest for your souls. For my yoke is easy to
bear, and the burden I give you is light."*

MATTHEW 11:28-30

Which way are you going? When fear and
anxiety are guiding your life, it's like strapping
yourself to a GPS that takes you to places
you don't want to go. Fear causes us to shrink back from
possibilities that could make a difference in our life.
Anxiety can cause us to react negatively when a helpful
hand is extended. So many times, these difficult emotions
are in the driver's seat.

In the passage above, Jesus offers to be your navigator.
He will provide a source of comfort in "his yoke," which
will bind you to him as he takes the lead. You will not go
it alone—rather, you will feel secure as he leads the way.
Jesus' assurance is that his way will be easy to bear and
the burden light.

The challenge you have is to trust Jesus with your life.
His invitation is for "all who are weary and carry heavy
burdens." Jesus is asking you to let him help you carry
the things that are weighing you down. Jesus will provide
soulful rest for you today and every day of your life.

Christ's invitation to the weary and heavy-laden is a call to begin life over again upon a new principle—upon His own principle. "Watch My way of doing things," He says. "Follow Me. Take life as I take it. Be meek and lowly and you will find Rest."

Henry Drummond

Once I knew what it was to rest upon the rock of God's promises, and it was indeed a precious resting place, but now I rest in His grace. He is teaching me that the bosom of His love is a far sweeter resting-place than even the rock of His promises.

Hannah Whitall Smith

In place of our exhaustion and spiritual fatigue, He will give us rest. All He asks is that we come to Him . . . that we spend a while thinking about Him, meditating on Him, talking to Him, listening in silence, occupying ourselves with Him—totally and thoroughly lost in the hiding place of His presence.

Chuck Swindoll

## FOR FURTHER REFLECTION

Psalm 23; Hebrews 4

### TODAY'S PRAYER

Lord Jesus, I come to you today and ask you to carry my load, knowing you will lead me in the way you desire. Please provide rest for my weary journey. Amen.

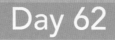

# Day 62

## Blessed Trust

*Blessed are those who trust in the LORD and
have made the LORD their hope and confidence.*

JEREMIAH 17:7

In a world that is image-conscious, overly concerned
with looks, success, and prosperity, it only stands
to reason that anxiety would be at an all-time high.
Never before in history has the focus on how we look,
other people's approval, and whether we are on the
"right" team been so important. We have the ability to see
ourselves on our phones, which are really cameras, and
we use them as internet portals to post our opinions and
highlight reels. We can use filters on our phones to make
ourselves look as though we have no flaws.

Viewing all the "happy face" pictures on social media
can make you feel that your life isn't as fun or exciting as
other people's. You may worry that you don't measure up.
This type of anxiety can keep building, and it sometimes
contributes to financial, physical, and emotional distress
as you try to maintain an image rather than be the real
you. We can project an image that looks like we have
it all figured out. However, it amounts to chasing after
acceptance from the world, which is not eternal.

This isn't to say that doing your best is wrong, but when
you are so focused on the opinions of this world, you can
lose sight of the One whose opinion can give you the
confidence you can rest your life upon. When you know

for certain that the Lord loves you and has a purpose for your life, it gives you the confidence to live life to the fullest! It is truly a blessing to trust the Lord for your approval and acceptance.

We don't need self-confidence, we need God-confidence.

Joyce Meyer

Most of us spend years chasing things in this world that we think will make us feel loved. But everything this world has to offer is temporary. Everything. The kind of love our souls crave is lasting, eternal. And only God can fill up our hearts with that kind of love.

Lysa TerKeurst

Oh, how great peace and quietness would he possess who should cut off all vain anxiety and place all his confidence in God.

Thomas à Kempis

## For further reflection

Isaiah 26:3; Proverbs 3:5-6; Romans 15:13

### TODAY'S PRAYER

Thank you, Lord, for your confidence in me! Help me to look to you for approval. Help me to be more like you. Amen.

# More

*Now all glory to God, who is able, through his mighty power at work within us, to accomplish infinitely more than we might ask or think.*

EPHESIANS 3:20

Panicky feelings can set in really quickly when things are not going the way you expected. You begin to feel afraid of what will happen next. Is there a way out? What should I do next? It's difficult to process those questions when your brain is so fired up. What can you do in moments like these? Breathe. Take a minute and breathe.

When you pause in the midst of panic, it can create some mental space so you can focus, problem-solve, and pray. Sometimes simple prayers—like "Help!"—can be so effective when we feel overwhelmed with anxiety. Panic attacks can feel like a heart attack, or like you cannot breathe, and it is important to ask for help to determine if anything physical is wrong. They can be debilitating and disruptive if they continue. The good news is there is help—panic attacks can be diminished with professional help.

Sometimes you need more space, more help, more peace. God will provide more than you might ask or think. Another translation of the passage from Ephesians says, "more than we might ask or imagine." The truth is, God is able. When we are feeling panicky, we can trust God with our needs, and he will provide.

Don't ever hesitate to take to God whatever is on your heart. He already knows it anyway, but He doesn't want you to bear its pain or celebrate its joy alone.

Billy Graham

When the Lord opens a door, walk through it. If He doesn't, just trust.

Kari Jobe

God's timing is always perfect. Trust His delays. He's got you.

Tony Evans

## For further reflection

Deuteronomy 31:8; Isaiah 40:31; Psalm 121:4-5

## TODAY'S PRAYER

Lord Jesus, thank you for your calming presence in my life! Help me to breathe when I want to hold my breath, help me to move when I feel stuck, and help me to recognize you are more than able to do more than I ask or imagine! Amen.

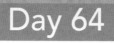

# Possibilities!

*Jesus looked at them intently and said, "Humanly speaking, it is impossible. But not with God. Everything is possible with God."*

MARK 10:27

Anxiety is born out of a sense of a loss of control, and our worry that some situation is going to end badly. Playing out all the options in your mind can multiply the anxiety! It's not realistic to think everything in your life will go as planned. You will face some situations where you cannot possibly know the outcome.

God has given each of us a brain and a free will to make choices as we please. We don't always use our brains to make wise choices. This usually creates anxiety as we experience the consequences of our choices.

But sometimes we feel anxious about a situation that wasn't our choice, and doesn't feel like it is part of God's will—and there isn't much we can do about it. At times like that, our brain needs to kick back into gear. We can remind ourselves that for God, all things are possible. God works in ways we cannot see and can work out things for our good. We can trust him with our concerns and our impossible situations. If you are facing something today that seems impossible to solve, trust God with it, knowing he will make a way.

God can do nothing for me until I recognize the limits of what is humanly possible, allowing Him to do the impossible.

Oswald Chambers

When life caves in, you do not need reasons—you need comfort. You do not need some answers--you need someone. And Jesus does not come to us with an explanation—He comes to us with His presence.

Bob Benson

I guess that sometimes, even when we can see something is very wrong, it doesn't mean that God isn't at work executing a much greater plan.

Patsy Clairmont

## FOR FURTHER REFLECTION
2 Corinthians 12:8-10; Psalm 145:18-19; James 1:12

### TODAY'S PRAYER

Heavenly Father, help me trust you with the impossible things in my life, knowing you are sovereign and are working on my behalf in every situation. Amen.

# Now Go!

*The LORD asked Moses, "Who makes a person's mouth? Who decides whether people speak or do not speak, hear or do not hear, see or do not see? Is it not I, the LORD? Now go! I will be with you as you speak, and I will instruct you in what to say."*

EXODUS 4:11-12

Have you ever felt frozen in fear or stuck in a cycle of anxiety? No amount of encouragement from anyone can pry you loose from the rigid state of your mind. What keeps you stuck? It could be self-doubt from previous experiences, a sense of insecurity about your capabilities, or just plain nervousness about trying something new.

This passage in scripture is so powerful because God had called Moses to lead the people out of slavery. Moses was quick to offer every excuse he could come up with to get out of being the leader. Yet at every turn, God reminded Moses that he was calling him to fulfill this role. In the verses above, God reminds Moses that he created him and would be with him as he led the people to the Promised Land.

God will be with you in every minute of your day. He will provide instructions for your life to fulfill the purpose for which he created you. If you feel like you cannot take the next step, turn to God to be assured that the One who calls you will lead you and be with you. You can trust in God's presence and will be able to move forward in your life.

God is the God of "right now." He doesn't want you sitting around regretting yesterday. Nor does He want you wringing your hands and worrying about the future. He wants you focusing on what He is saying to you and putting in front of you . . . right now.

Priscilla Shirer

Courage isn't a feeling that you wait for. Courage is doing when you don't have courage. Courage is doing it scared.

Jill Briscoe

We are all faced with a series of great opportunities brilliantly disguised as impossible situations.

Chuck Swindoll

## FOR FURTHER REFLECTION

Philippians 4:13; Jeremiah 29:11;
2 Chronicles 20:15-17

## TODAY'S PRAYER

Lord, I am willing to go where you lead.
Help me have courage to trust that
you will go with me and that you have
a purpose for my life. For your glory!
Amen.

## Safekeeping

*The LORD keeps you from all harm and watches over your life. The LORD keeps watch over you as you come and go, both now and forever.*

PSALM 121:7-8

When you are rattled with fear and worry, remember God is keeping you safe. We tend to overlook that simple truth when we are consumed with the things of this life. Whether you just heard some bad news or are wrestling with an ongoing tough situation, God is with you.

One reason we overlook this promise from God is that in troubling times it seems so far from our hearts and minds. How can we recall this great promise when we are struggling? We need to read it—to literally put our eyes on these words of scripture. Our minds need renewing, and for that to happen we need to meditate on these words. When we can focus on the promises of God, we are reassured of the truth.

Whatever you are focused on in this season of life, be reminded that the Lord watches over you and knows your needs. This promise is eternal, forevermore. Let these words sink into your heart and mind today.

Worry does not empty tomorrow of its sorrows; it empties today of its strength.

Corrie ten Boom

We can trust God with all our problems, all our heartaches, and especially with all our long-term anxieties. Every morning as we wake ourselves up with a splash of joy we can say, "WHATEVER, LORD!"

Barbara Johnson

It is good to remind ourselves that the will of God comes from the heart of God and that we need not be afraid.

Warren Wiersbe

## FOR FURTHER REFLECTION

Isaiah 43:1-3; Romans 8:28; Psalm 32:7

### TODAY'S PRAYER

Heavenly Father, thank you for your safekeeping of my heart! Help me to rest in your shelter and be strengthened by your love. Amen.

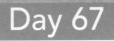

# Be Bold!

*Let us come boldly to the throne of our gracious God.*
*There we will receive his mercy, and we will*
*find grace to help us when we need it most.*

Hebrews 4:16

Hesitancy is part of life for many people. You may not feel quite sure about situations you are in, decisions you have to make, or your relationships. Everything feels risky—you might want to take something on, but at the same time have to muscle through your own resistance.

Sometimes hesitancy in our day-to-day life is due to fear and anxiety. It is an ever-present reality that we push through. Many people around us would be surprised if they knew what was going on inside of us: the constant chatter or hum of insecurity or questioning about every step we take. It isn't easy to turn off, and it is frustrating to never have a moment of peace.

When you feel hesitant, be bold and ask God for strength to push through it. Quiet your heart and mind and ask God for clarity about your daily life. Sensing God's presence even when you face challenging decisions or relationship struggles can encourage you to boldly persevere. "Boldly" isn't the same as "rudely." It's about a sense of strength and assurance—knowing you are able because God is with you. What do you need to be bold about in your requests to God?

Courage comes from a heart that is CONVINCED it is loved.

Beth Moore

We need never shout across the spaces to an absent God. He is nearer than our own soul, closer than our most secret thoughts.

A. W. Tozer

Jesus tends to his people individually. He personally sees to our needs. We all receive Jesus' touch. We experience his care.

Max Lucado

## For further reflection

Psalm 55:22; 1 Peter 5:10; Colossians 3:23-24

### TODAY'S PRAYER

Thank you, Lord, for your availability! Help me to ask you for all that I need, knowing you will provide. You are a faithful God and have the strength I need for each day. Amen.

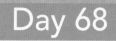

## Your Time

*"If you keep quiet at a time like this, deliverance
and relief for the Jews will arise from some
other place, but you and your relatives will die.
Who knows if perhaps you were made queen
for just such a time as this?"*

ESTHER 4:14

The account of Esther in the Old Testament tells of the salvation of the Jews by a young woman who has been placed in a leadership role, but doesn't feel like much of a leader. She has great support from her uncle, who is distressed over the threat of the annihilation of their people. In this verse, he is telling her that it is her time to take a stand for her people. He reminds her that she has been given this role in their kingdom. Even though she feels uncertain, Esther chooses to do what she can to make a move. It was her time.

In our battle with uncertainty in our own lives, we wrestle with indecision. Especially when the stakes are high or there is risk involved, we may feel insecure and doubt that we can make a difference. We seek out opinions, pray and ask God what to do, and still it is up to us to make the move. Have you been there? It can feel like you are walking a tightrope—one bad step and it's over.

The good news is, God's got you. He has equipped you with insight and knowledge for the situations you face. Through prayer, good counsel, and your own experiences, God has a plan for you to make a difference in your world. Think back on your life: you have already survived every decision you have made up to this point! Our uncertainty keeps us from stepping onto the path God has for our lives. He wants you to participate in his plan, and that plan will be a blessing to you and those in your sphere of influence.

God has a plan for all of us, but He expects us to do our share of the work.

Minnie Pearl

I believe that God has a plan and purpose not only for the human race, but for my individual life.

Anne Graham Lotz

Trusting God's plan is the only secret I know in the gentle art of not freaking out.

Lysa TerKeurst

## FOR FURTHER REFLECTION

Jeremiah 29:11; Psalm 32:8; Hebrews 13:20-21

### TODAY'S PRAYER

Lord Jesus, may I feel your strength as I make decisions in my life, so that my choices will honor your plan for me and you will be glorified in my life. Thank you for your purpose for my life. Amen.

# Balance

*We are pressed on every side by troubles, but we are not crushed. We are perplexed, but not driven to despair. We are hunted down, but never abandoned by God. We get knocked down, but we are not destroyed.*

2 CORINTHIANS 4:8-9

Are you a catastrophic thinker? Do you usually expect the worst? To some extent this may be because your experience or training have given you insight, and you can see the potential danger in a situation. Your perspective tends to be negative, but your rationale is that bad things do happen so it's better to be prepared.

The downside of this mindset is that negativity affects you in other ways. It can keep you from experiencing life in the moment as you are forever looking towards what could happen. However, there is good that can come from your insight and knowledge—put to good use, it can help your family and make the world a better place. Balance is the key. As you consider what could go wrong, also consider what good things could happen. Best-case scenarios can provide the inspiration for solutions.

This passage is an example of balance. The apostle Paul is sharing that we will experience worst-case scenarios in this life, but we will never be abandoned by God! If you find yourself out of balance—thinking only of the worst-case scenario—spend time thinking about what good could come out of the situation that is on your mind. God will provide strength and courage as you consider the best that could happen in any situation.

Vision is the ability to see God's presence, to perceive God's power, to focus on God's plan in spite of the obstacles.

Chuck Swindoll

Circumstances may appear to wreck our lives and God's plans, but God is not helpless among the ruins. Our broken lives are not lost or useless. God's love is still working. He comes in and takes the calamity and uses it victoriously, working out His wonderful plan of love.

Eric Liddell

Hope doesn't announce that life is safe, therefore, we will be; instead, it whispers that Christ is our safety in the midst of harsh reality.

Patsy Clairmont

## For further reflection

2 Corinthians 10:3-5; Psalm 91; Proverbs 3:5-6

### TODAY'S PRAYER

Lord, help me to know you are working in all things. Help me to view the world I live in through your eyes and know that you will be with me even in the worst situations. Help me to see the good in each day, and your purpose. Amen.

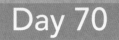
# Cared For

*He will feed his flock like a shepherd. He will carry*
*the lambs in his arms, holding them close to his heart.*
*He will gently lead the mother sheep with their young.*

ISAIAH 40:11

Many times, when we experience anxiety we are feeling the stress of life. We may feel exhausted by the effort we put forth each day. We may be concerned about how we will make ends meet. We may feel alone in our journey. When we wake up we feel dread for the day ahead. Sometimes this is free-floating, not based on anything specific, but the feeling is real.

Research indicates that when we are experiencing anxiety, we will find relief when we extend care towards someone else. The simple act of caring for another relieves our own feelings of anxiety. It doesn't need to cost anything—simply connecting through an email or text can encourage someone who may need to know you are thinking about them or praying for them. Maybe ask a neighbor if they need help with anything. You might not feel like you have the energy to extend care to another person, but if you will consider this action it may make the difference in your day.

The Lord cares for you. On days when you are weighed down by concern, recall the ways that God has provided for you. Express gratitude. Try keeping a journal with a list of things you are thankful for. You can also create a list of ways to help others, so that even when you feel stressed out you will have reminders of ways you could extend a helping hand. In this way you will literally be the hands and feet of Jesus, which will bring you peace.

It's understandable that we sometimes think the world's problems are so big that we can do little to help. On our own, we cannot end wars or wipe out injustice, but the cumulative impact of thousands of small acts of goodness can be bigger than we imagine.

Queen Elizabeth II

Nothing exalts the soul, gives it a sheer sense of buoyancy and victory, so much as the fact that we are being used to change the lives of other people.

E. Stanley Jones

It is one of the most beautiful compensations of this life that no man can sincerely try to help another without helping himself.

Ralph Waldo Emerson

## FOR FURTHER REFLECTION
Luke 6:38; Matthew 25:35-40; John 15:13

## TODAY'S PRAYER

Lord Jesus, thank you for your loving care for me. Help me to recognize the needs of others and equip me to fulfill your desire to help them. I ask for your peace of mind as I recognize you have given me all I need. Amen.

# God of All

*"I am the LORD, the God of all the peoples of the world. Is anything too hard for me?"*

JEREMIAH 32:27

Are you a control freak? Here is a gentler way to put it: do you feel like your life would be so much better if you could have more of a say in how things go? Control is a big component of anxiety. When we feel like we have control, we tend to feel less anxious. The problem is, to really experience true peace we have to surrender control. How exactly is that supposed to help us feel less anxious? As we practice surrendering control, we learn to discern where we actually can have control in our life.

There are some things we simply have to accept. That doesn't necessarily mean we agree with the issue; it means we acknowledge the reality of the situation. Can you recognize when you are acting as if you control everything, and not accepting things as they are? Sometimes it is revealed in our defensiveness, anger, short-tempered responses, and lack of openness to alternative suggestions. When we are able to surrender control, we begin to accept reality. Then we can use our experience, knowledge, education, and gifts to make wise decisions. As we practice surrender, we experience peace, knowing God is sovereign and will help us through any situation we may face in our life.

When we know that God is working in every situation, we can accept things as they are, be curious as we seek ways to work for good, and experience peace as we surrender to his will. No one wants to be a freak of any kind! As you recognize the areas you are seeking to control, ask God to reveal the way of surrender to you and experience his peace.

Acceptance is the answer to all my problems today. When I am disturbed, it is because I find some person, place, thing, or situation—some fact of my life— unacceptable to me. I can find no serenity until I accept that person, place, thing, or situation as being exactly the way it is supposed to be at this moment.

Alcoholics Anonymous

We have little control over the circumstances of life. We can't control the weather or the economy, and we can't control what other people say about or do to us. There is only one area where we have control--we can rule the kingdom inside. The heart of every problem is the problem in the heart.

Warren Wiersbe

## For further reflection

Colossians 3:15-17; Romans 15:1-7; Matthew 6:25-32

### TODAY'S PRAYER

Lord God, you are the maker of heaven and earth. Nothing is too hard for you! Help me surrender my need to control, knowing that your way is the best. Provide insight as I live my life in your will for your glory. Amen.

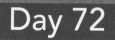

# Talking to Yourself

*May the words of my mouth and the meditation*
*of my heart be pleasing to you, O Lord,*
*my rock and my redeemer.*

PSALM 19:14

Are you in the habit of putting yourself down? When you make a mistake, do you call yourself an "idiot" or "stupid"? For some people it's a lifelong habit. Let's decide to end that practice today.

It is powerful for you to hear your voice in your own ears, no matter what you hear yourself saying. Whether it is something negative about yourself or a situation, or a message of fear, or of hope, you tend to believe what you say. Stop for a minute and think about what you hear yourself saying. Are you loving? Kind? Helpful? Or do you tend to be sarcastic, negative, and judgmental? The scriptures talk about how what is in our hearts is revealed in our speech.

You may not realize how your own voice may be ratcheting up your level of anxiety, worry, fears, and concerns. Begin today to be aware of what you are saying. When you make a mistake or are confronted by something unexpected, take a minute before responding. Listen to your own voice and you will begin to recognize the ways in which you may or may not be saying what is true. Focus on expressing truth and uplifting others. Look for the good in every situation and what will honor God. It is a good habit to cultivate!

Evidence is conclusive that your self-talk has a direct bearing on your performance.

Zig Ziglar

Put your own oxygen mask on first. I watch the self-talk that goes through my mind, and if I am being critical with myself, I shake myself out of it.

Anne Lamott

Thoughts, positive or negative, grow stronger when fertilized with constant repetition.

Chuck Swindoll

## For further reflection

Psalm 103:1-5; Proverbs 4:23; Philippians 4:8-9

### TODAY'S PRAYER

Lord Jesus, as I speak help me to be mindful of what I say. Help me to be loving, kind, and gracious to myself and others. As I seek your Word, may truth be revealed in my life. Amen.

# Day 73

## Peace

*I have told you all this so that you may have peace
in me. Here on earth you will have many trials
and sorrows. But take heart, because
I have overcome the world.*

JOHN 16:33

In this passage Jesus is speaking directly to the disciples as he is preparing them for his departure from their presence. You may need to hear this message today. Perhaps you are feeling afraid of what the day will bring, or you may be unsure of a decision you need to make. It's interesting that Jesus doesn't say we will not experience fear or anxiety; what he promises is that he has overcome anything this world may bring into our lives.

In the midst of your fear, ask the Lord to bring peace to your heart and mind. No matter what you are facing today, Christ is able to provide the peace that will allow you to move through the challenge with confidence. This doesn't guarantee that you won't experience strong feelings of fear; it means you won't be alone.

As long as you live there will be some challenges you will go through. That doesn't mean that you will be alone in whatever trial comes your way. It doesn't mean you somehow aren't "good enough" to prevent it from happening. It means that none of us are living in the Garden as we were designed, and sin will have its effect on our world through disease, struggles, relationship issues, and more. We can overcome through the power of Christ and his resurrection at work in our lives. Your peace comes from Christ no matter what you're facing today.

In any trial, in any bitter situation, you are not alone, you are not helpless, you are not a victim. You have a tree, a cross, shown to you by the Sovereign God of Calvary. Whatever the trial or temptation, it is not more than you can bear. It is bearable. It can be handled. You can know as Joseph knew, "You meant evil against me, but God meant it for good in order to bring about this present result, to preserve many people alive" (Genesis 50:20).

Kay Arthur

Many times, Christians face trials and suffering simply because we live in a world full of sin.

Joyce Meyer

## FOR FURTHER REFLECTION

Psalm 4; Daniel 10:19; Proverbs 3:1-4

### TODAY'S PRAYER

Lord Jesus, I am in need of your peace today. Help me as I move in your power to deal with the issues I face, knowing you are over all of them. Help me to live in this world knowing you are always present with me, for your glory. Amen.

# Listen and Understand

*To those who listen to my teaching, more understanding will be given, and they will have an abundance of knowledge. But for those who are not listening, even what little understanding they have will be taken away from them.*

MATTHEW 13:12

D id you know that anxiety affects your brain? It seems obvious, doesn't it? When we are feeling anxious it actually disrupts our ability to think well. Think about the last time you were feeling anxious and you might recall that it clouded your thoughts. The reality is that we will not go through life without anxiety—it is part of our human experience. It actually is part of our brain function to alert us to danger or stressful situations.

Sometimes we get so stressed about feeling anxious that we literally cannot shift our thinking in another direction. We have to learn how to recognize and manage anxiety when it occurs, and when to seek help. The good news is that we can learn how to deal with and manage our anxiety. The first step is to acknowledge when you are experiencing the anxiety—you can simply say, "I feel anxious." There may not be a way to resolve it immediately, but just acknowledging how you are feeling can actually bring some relief.

The teachings of Jesus are so helpful as we navigate times of anxiety. We can rest on his promises that he will always be with us and will provide insight and strength. Spend time reading the promises of Christ and make it part of your daily practice. When anxiety does come, you will be reminded of truths that will provide peace of mind.

Someone once said, "The best way to forget your troubles is to wear tight shoes." I'd like to add that high heels can do the job just as well.

Patsy Clairmont

The little troubles and worries of life may be as stumbling blocks in our way, or we may make them stepping-stones to a nobler character and to Heaven. Troubles are often the tools by which God fashions us for better things.

Henry Ward Beecher

As you walk through the valley of the unknown, you will find the footprints of Jesus both in front of you and beside you.

Charles Stanley

## For further reflection

2 Timothy 1:6-7; Philippians 4:6-9; 1 Peter 1:6-9

### TODAY'S PRAYER

Lord Jesus, please help me today when my anxious thoughts want to take over my thinking. Give me clarity and assurance of your presence. Help me to remember your promises each day. Amen.

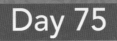

# Day 75

## Instructions

*Be on guard. Stand firm in the faith. Be courageous.*
*Be strong. And do everything with love.*

1 Corinthians 16:13-14

When fear has you in its grip and you are not sure of what to do, it would be helpful to have a set of instructions on how to be brave! Something like driver's ed, when you had the teacher in the passenger seat (with their own personal brake pedal!) calmly giving you instructions about how to merge onto the highway. The first time behind the wheel is pretty scary!

The first part of this passage is all about strength and boldness, followed by "and do everything with love"— which is usually equated with gentleness and grace. You don't have to put on a brave front to address your fears. You may have seen this acronym for "fear": False Evidence Appearing Real. However, some fears aren't false. Receiving a scary diagnosis—that's real. Maybe you lost your job—that's scary and real, too. The idea isn't to ignore your fear, or deny it, but rather to acknowledge the fear and then follow the instructions that are in this scripture.

Today if fear wants to be in the driver's seat, remember these instructions as you hang onto the steering wheel. Fear is real, but it doesn't have to take over your life.

The presence of fear does not mean you have no faith. Fear visits everyone. But make your fear a visitor and not a resident.

Max Lucado

Whatever has you afraid, angry, intimidated or frustrated tonight—take it to our all-powerful and all-capable God. He has the answer.

Lysa TerKeurst

One of the greatest discoveries a man makes, one of his great surprises, is to find he can do what he was afraid he couldn't do.

Henry Ford

## For further reflection

John 14:27; Isaiah 41:10; Psalm 27:13-14

## TODAY'S PRAYER

Thank you, Lord, for your strength and grace. Help me to focus on your truth when I am afraid. I pray for your courage and love to guide me. Amen.

# Humble Down

*Humble yourselves, therefore, under God's mighty hand, that he may lift you up in due time. Cast all your anxiety on him because he cares for you.*

1 PETER 5:6-7 NIV

Fear and anxiety are manifested in different ways in different people. Our human emotions are so unique to each of us, and that is a beautiful thing! Fear and anxiety cause some people to be angry, defensive, and agitated, and some others to be withdrawn, depressed, and tearful. There is no single way these emotions are expressed. That is why it is important to recognize if you are developing a pattern in your emotions that may indicate you are feeling fear, anxiety, or both.

Sometimes we don't recognize we need help until we are confronted by a loved one who may be concerned, or who may have been in your path on a bad day. Has anyone told you they are worried about you? Perhaps you have had an issue at work or in a personal relationship in which you reacted so strongly that others distanced themselves from you. Humble down and recognize that you might need help figuring out what is at the core of your anxiety and fears.

God provides people to help us in our life. Sometimes we pride ourselves on being able to handle everything life throws at us, but we are not created to go it alone. Recognize your need and connect with a group, friend, counselor, or pastor to release whatever is driving your fear and anxiety. Pray, asking God to show you what is wrong. Surrender your fear and anxiety to him and trust that he will lead you into freedom.

You don't always have the power to control, but you always have the power to surrender.

Craig Groeschel

Fear is the needle that pierces us that it may carry a thread to bind us to heaven.

James Hastings

The meek man will attain a place of soul rest. As he walks on in meekness, he will be happy to let God defend him. The old struggle to defend himself is over. He has found the peace which meekness brings.

A. W. Tozer

## For further reflection

Colossians 3:12-17; Ephesians 4:1-7; Micah 6:8

## TODAY'S PRAYER

Heavenly Father, help me have insight about what is in my heart. Please reveal the unsurrendered places in my life. Thank you for your loving care for me. Amen.

# Hope

*I pray that God, the source of hope, will fill you completely with joy and peace because you trust in him. Then you will overflow with confident hope through the power of the Holy Spirit.*

ROMANS 15:13

Anxiety and fear undercut our hope and can make it difficult to keep a positive attitude and believe that things will get better. Concerns swirling in our mind distract us from our present reality, consuming our energy and depleting our reserves. It literally can keep you from getting out of bed.

Sound familiar? Perhaps this is where you are now. If so, take a breath, literally—breathe in for three seconds, hold it for three, and then exhale for three. When we are feeling anxious and fearful, we have a tendency to take shallow breaths, or even hold our breath, Our bodies react to the stress we carry inside. Physical exercise like taking a run or a walk outside can help alleviate the stress, renew our energy, and reclaim our focus.

If you are overwhelmed and your worries and fears are taking over the better part of your day, please seek help. Reach out to a friend, call a therapist, or see your doctor. Help yourself feel better. There is hope and help available for you.

Most of the important things in the world have been accomplished by people who have kept on trying when there seemed to be no hope at all.

Dale Carnegie

Hope begins in the dark, the stubborn hope that if you just show up and try to do the right thing, the dawn will come. You wait and watch and work: You don't give up.

Anne Lamott

What gives me the most hope every day is God's grace; knowing that his grace is going to give me the strength for whatever I face, knowing that nothing is a surprise to God.

Rick Warren

## FOR FURTHER REFLECTION

Isaiah 40:31; 2 Corinthians 4:16-18;
Hebrews 10:23-25

### TODAY'S PRAYER

Lord Jesus, I am in need of hope today. I am struggling and I know you are the One who can help me. Thank you for your strength and courage as I look to you for help. Amen.

# Day 78

# Truth

*You belong to God, my dear children. You have
already won a victory over those people, because
the Spirit who lives in you is greater than
the spirit who lives in the world.*

1 JOHN 4:4

You are not alone in your battle with fear or
anxiety, even though you might feel as though
you are fighting without any help. Our feelings
are powerful—but they are not always true. That may
seem surprising, because in our world feelings are what is
deemed to be truth. Our feelings are important, but they
are not truth.

Feelings are expressions of someone's emotional or
physical state. If you look the word up in the dictionary
the definition doesn't mention truth. This isn't to
dismiss the validity and experience of feelings—but it is
a reminder that feelings are not always good at giving
directions for your life. For example, a young child may
have fears at night, and as her parents reassure her that
there is nothing to be afraid of, they are able to calm her
fears. That doesn't negate the child's feelings; it adds truth
to her feelings, so she is comforted.

Are your feelings your GPS? Are they taking you down
winding roads and dead-end streets? Do you feel as
though you have no one to share your feelings with who
could help you to discover what is true? The Holy Spirit is
always with us to guide us into truth. Pray for

discernment, seek God's truth in the Bible, and connect with godly friends who can provide support for your journey.

When we talk about the peace of God, don't think of singing and swaying and holding hands in a circle. The peace of God is strong, intense, palpable, real. You can sense its stable presence giving you inner security despite insecure circumstances.

Priscilla Shirer

Though our feelings come and go, His love for us does not.

C. S. Lewis

Remember that we cannot judge the moral value of any action by how we feel. Our feelings are unreliable and cannot be trusted to convey truth.

Joyce Meyer

## FOR FURTHER REFLECTION

Proverbs 17:22; Ephesians 2:1-10; Isaiah 58:11

## TODAY'S PRAYER

Lord Jesus, help me discern truth through your Holy Spirit. Thank you for your guidance. Help me to follow you. Amen.

# God's Purpose

*Yes, I am the gate. Those who come in through me will be saved. . . . The thief's purpose is to steal and kill and destroy. My purpose is to give them a rich and satisfying life.*

JOHN 10:9-10

All of us experience challenging times. We all have different ways of navigating through really difficult seasons—we ask for help, pray, hunker down until it passes, or a combination of all of these strategies. In difficult times, we need reminding that God is with us no matter what the circumstance. We also need to know that we have an enemy of our soul that wants us to lose our trust that God is with us, doubt that anything good can come from our trial, and give up. Confusion sets in when we lose sight of the truth that God is with us.

When we believe that everything should be wonderful because we love Jesus, we forget that we still live in a broken world. The redemption of the world through Jesus' death and resurrection is the power at work in our lives. That is what we can be sure of in uncertain times. The promise of a rich and satisfying life includes the times that you have overcome a difficult season, the strength you've had to endure losses, and the peace that passes understanding in the challenges you have survived.

For clarity in your life, remember Jesus' promise in John 10:10. Every time you see a digital clock display 10:10, let it be a reminder that there is hope and the promise of a life that is full! Be encouraged today that the Lord has overcome!

Don't quit, and don't give up. The reward is just around the corner. And in times of doubt or times of joy, listen for that still, small voice. Know that God has been there from the beginning—and he will be there until . . . The End.

Joanna Gaines

Cruelty and wrong are not the greatest forces in the world. There is nothing eternal in them. Only love is eternal.

Elisabeth Elliot

When I understand that everything that is happening to me is to make me more Christlike, it resolves a great deal of anxiety.

A. W. Tozer

## For further reflection

Proverbs 3:5-6; John 13:7; Romans 8:26-30

### TODAY'S PRAYER

Lord Jesus, help me in my challenging time. I know that you will work in the midst of the trouble and provide a way. Help me to know when the enemy is attacking and to be strong in my faith that you will work all things for my good. Amen.

# Reassurance

*"Fear not; you will no longer live in shame.*
*Don't be afraid; there is no more disgrace for you.*
*You will no longer remember the shame of*
*your youth and the sorrows of widowhood."*

Isaiah 54:4

We have an amazing ability to remember negative comments, bad experiences, and devastating losses. It's as though our past is streaming on a big screen right in front of us, replaying the choices and events that rocked our world. How can we go on living if we carry these burdens with us? Will there ever be relief?

Anxiety and fear have roots in so many experiences in our lives. We live in a broken world and not one of us can claim perfection. The good news is that God sees us in our brokenness, and in his love he offers healing and comfort. We can rest in the promises that are throughout scripture. His reassurance of redemption, grace, and mercy for each of us will give us the strength to move forward and experience freedom from the past.

Is there something in your past that is shaking your present? No matter what happened to you, no matter what choice you made, allow the peace of God to calm your heart and mind with the truth of his Word. God loves you and is with you. He sees you and knows your needs. You can trust that he has forgiven you. He will bind up your wounds and set you free to live your life for his glory.

To pray is to accept that we are, and always will be, wholly dependent on God for everything.

Timothy Keller

Tomorrow's freedom is today's surrender.

Stuart Gerrard, David Leonard, and Leslie Jordan

If you think you've blown God's plan for your life, rest in this: you are not that powerful.

Lisa Bevere

## FOR FURTHER REFLECTION

Psalm 138:8; 2 Corinthians 4; Psalm 61

### TODAY'S PRAYER

Lord, you know all of my days and have a purpose for each one. Help me to live this day knowing that you have covered my past and have given me hope for my future. Amen.

# Mountain Mover

*Jesus said to the disciples, "Have faith in God.
I tell you the truth, you can say to this mountain,
'May you be lifted up and thrown into the sea,'
and it will happen. But you must really believe
it will happen and have no doubt in your heart."*

MARK 11:22-23

There are days when anxiety feels like a mountain sitting on top of you—like you are pinned down and unable to move. On days when it is clear to you what you are worried about it, you can make some sense of your thoughts. On some other days, though, anxiety may not be specific, just invasive, which can feel overwhelming. We try to understand the root cause but meanwhile still feel that mountain. So frustrating.

This passage of scripture confuses some people. Can we really move mountains? Is it just as simple as believing and then it will happen? If you have wondered about this, you aren't alone. Of course, we want the mountains to be moved—especially when they are sitting on top of us! What Jesus is telling the disciples—and us—is to trust God with the mountains. We can ask him, in faith, to remove a challenge, knowing he will. The way this works isn't simple; nothing we are experiencing is simple. However, when we are able to trust and just do as God says, we experience a simple truth—God is faithful in all things.

The challenge is to trust God. Simply have faith, ask for what you need, and believe it will happen. Know that God is working in your life, that he loves you and will provide for your needs. God will indeed move your mountain.

Sometimes when we get overwhelmed we forget how big God is.

A. W. Tozer

There comes a moment when you must quit talking to God about the mountain in your life and start talking to the mountain about your God.

Mark Batterson

My Saviour, He can move the mountains, My God is Mighty to save, He is Mighty to save.

Reuben Morgan and Ben Fielding

## For further reflection

Exodus 14:13-14; Psalm 73:23-26; Nahum 1:5

### TODAY'S PRAYER

Lord God, you have the power to remove my mountains. Help me to trust you with all that weighs me down and know without a doubt you are able to remove the challenges in my life. Help me to do as you ask, knowing you have a plan for me. Amen.

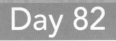

# Confidence

*We are always confident, even though we
know that as long as we live in these bodies
we are not at home with the Lord. For we
live by believing and not by seeing.*

2 Corinthians 5:6-7

If you have watched the news lately, you are probably
feeling a bit more anxious. The media reports the
news in a manner to grab your attention—and with
so many things in our world that are scary, that it isn't
difficult. We cannot live in denial of all that is going on or
avoid knowing of the heartache that is in the world. God
is working in our lives to make a difference in the world
as we bring his message to the lost.

When you feel insecure about life, wondering how things
will turn out in your relationships, career, or ministry,
remember the hope you have in Christ. He is working
all things to the good, and there is much to do! You can
be confident that God sees what is happening. You can
be confident that he is moving in the hearts and minds
of believers. We are not always able to see how he is
working, though. We have to build our trust and faith that
God is working in all things.

If your confidence is lacking, ask God today to provide
courage for whatever you are facing. Believe that he is
able and will help you as you bravely move forward. The
Lord goes before you every step of the way.

Today is what the Lord has prepared you for.

Mark Dever

Down through the centuries in times of trouble and trial God has brought courage to the hearts of those who love Him. The Bible is filled with assurances of God's help and comfort in every kind of trouble which might cause fears to arise in the human heart.

Billy Graham

We are . . . presented with a door that leads into a country that is not our own, a foreign land hostile to our message, our mission, and our King. Yet it also longs for the very thing Jesus provides. So we walk out the door and into the world, armed with the gospel of grace and strengthened through fervent prayer to God's Spirit, who gives us compassion, and through God's church, which gives us community.

Ed Stetzer

## FOR FURTHER REFLECTION

Jeremiah 17:7-8; Deuteronomy 31:6-8; John 14:27

## TODAY'S PRAYER

Thank you, Lord Jesus, for the knowledge that you are always with me. You will give me confidence to follow your will and to share your love with others so that I might fulfill your calling on my life, for your glory. Amen.

# Heard

*In my distress, I cried out to the LORD; yes,*
*I prayed to my God for help. He heard me from*
*his sanctuary; my cry to him reached his ears.*

PSALM 18:6

One of the most valuable elements in any relationship is to feel like you are heard. When conversations escalate to raised voices, it usually indicates that the people in the conversation do not believe they are being heard. Did that sentence make you think of a conversation you were part of that was like that? It can be so very frustrating to feel as though your requests go unheard.

When we don't feel heard, anxiety and fears can develop. You may feel as though you don't matter and what you have to say isn't valuable. The anxiety and fear we feel usually causes anger, hurt, disappointment, and distance. Many people in relationships struggle with the issue of listening well. If they seek help there can be a better resolution to the problem.

What if you don't feel like God hears you? The psalmist expresses himself like this: "I cried out to the Lord." Have you felt like you couldn't be open and honest with God about your anxieties and fears? Do you feel like you have to use eloquent religious phrases for your prayers to be proper? You don't. God hears you in your whispers and in your shouts. God provides the Holy Spirit to help you pray about things you cannot bear to share. Today, you can be sure that the Lord hears you—and wants to hear from you. Will you share your heart with God today?

The right way to approach God is to stretch out our hands and ask of One who we know has the heart of a Father.

Dietrich Bonhoeffer

Prayer delights God's ear, it melts His heart, it opens His hand: God cannot deny a praying soul.

Thomas Watson

The greatest tragedy of life is not unanswered prayer, but unoffered prayer.

F. B. Meyer

## For further reflection

Proverbs 15:29; Romans 8:26; 1 John 5:14

## TODAY'S PRAYER

Thank you, God, for hearing me so well!
I know that I can bring you all of my fears
and worries, knowing you are listening.
Amen.

# Connected

*I want them to be encouraged and knit together*
*by strong ties of love. I want them to have complete*
*confidence that they understand God's mysterious*
*plan, which is Christ himself.*

COLOSSIANS 2:2

Who is on your team? These are the people you go to when you need help with something, or just need to be held. You can be honest and open with them no matter what. If you don't have a team, is there a person you can trust with your anxiety and fear? We are created for connection, yet so many of us do not have people who are part of our team.

When we experience anxiety, we can be fearful of letting anyone know what is really going on in our life. That leads to a sense of isolation. Sometimes we feel like we need to be stronger—we even shame ourselves, thinking we should know how to deal with a particular problem. One of the most important things we can do in times of anxiety is to reach out and ask for help. You can build a team of people from different parts of your life to help you stay connected. Being connected is essential to your well-being.

Creating a team of safe people who you can trust and be open with may also bring you some anxiety. You might be feeling a bit awkward about asking someone to be there for you. Start by assessing who is already on your team. Perhaps you could serve on their team, too. Make it a priority to create connections and experience the support that is so vital to your well-being.

There are still days I need a hand-up from another journeyer. And there are still days I want to hide, since every season of life brings its set of threats, yet because of God's mercy and grace, I press on.

Patsy Clairmont

The soul needs to interact with other people to be healthy.

Donald Miller

My deepest hunger was my longing for connectedness and friendship.

Margaret Feinberg

## FOR FURTHER REFLECTION

1 John 4:7; Proverbs 27:17; Galatians 6:2

### TODAY'S PRAYER

Heavenly Father, help me to have godly connections with people who will journey with me. I know you created me for connection with you and with people who share my life. Thank you for your loving care for me through other people. Amen.

# Relief

*Strengthen those who have tired hands, and
encourage those who have weak knees. Say to
those with fearful hearts, "Be strong, and do not fear,
for your God is coming to destroy your enemies.
He is coming to save you."*

ISAIAH 35:3-4

If you have been dealing with anxiety or fear for any length of time, you are looking for relief. It drains your energy to have tensions and concerns as the operating system for your life. Negative suspicions that "nothing will get any better" spin off lots of questions, and that tires you out, which in turn creates more anxiety.

Wouldn't it be great to have some relief? To rest from carrying what seems like the stress of all the world? Relief is possible, but it will take some getting used to. When you begin to slow down you will feel the space that peace provides. And if you have been in a cycle of anxious thoughts for any length of time, you may be tempted to pick up where you left off. It kept you occupied. You may not know what to do with the peace you will experience. You will need a new routine.

When you begin to experience relief, lean into God's plan, trusting that anything you are worried about has already been dealt with in his timing and plan. You will discover a new way of life: Courage will replace fear as you move forward!

Patience is the ability to idle your motor when you feel like stripping your gears.

Barbara Johnson

No matter what I feel, I hold the assurance that God never leaves me.

Craig Groeschel

Make friends with your needs. Welcome them. They are a gift from God, designed to draw you into relationship with him and with his safe people. Your needs are the cure to the sin of self-sufficiency.

Henry Cloud and John Townsend

## FOR FURTHER REFLECTION

Matthew 11:28-30; Psalm 34:18; Romans 8:26-28

## TODAY'S PRAYER

Lord Jesus, I am in need of relief today. Help me lean on your strength and wisdom for my life. Help me as I find the rhythm of peace in my life. Amen.

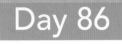

# Attentive

*I love the LORD because he hears my voice and my
prayer for mercy. Because he bends down to listen,
I will pray as long as I have breath!*

PSALM 116:1-2

God cares about you! He knows you because he
created you with his purpose and design. Even
in times when you feel uncertain, you can be
assured that God is attentive to your needs. Your fear and
anxiety may lead you to believe that God doesn't know
what you are experiencing. It simply is not true.

The truth is that God knows what you are going through
and wants to hear from you. When you begin the practice
of praying about what is making you afraid or causing you
anxiety, you will experience God's peace in his presence.
When we praise God in the midst of our struggle we will
feel his presence, which will calm our fears.

This isn't a magic formula. It is a spiritual practice.
God will meet you in the places where you need him
most. It could be a prayer in a doctor's office as you
wait for a diagnosis. It could be in your workplace when
deadlines are looming. It could be in your home, where
relationships are tense. Wherever you are, God will hear
your prayers and meet you with grace and mercy.

Hope is the expectation of fulfillment that is anchored in God's promise to meet my need. Hope is not based on my emotional or mental determination. It is rooted in God. Quite simply, we are optimistic because we have faith in whom we have placed our hope.

Marilyn Meberg

The function of prayer is not to influence God, but rather to change the nature of the one who prays.

Søren Kierkegaard

## FOR FURTHER REFLECTION

1 John 5:14-15; Psalm 102:17; Romans 12:12

### TODAY'S PRAYER

Lord Jesus, I lift my heart to you today—
all my concerns, fears, and challenges.
I know you will hear my prayer and meet
my needs. Thank you for your grace and
mercy. Amen.

# Security

*I know the LORD is always with me. I will
not be shaken, for he is right beside me.*

PSALM 16:8

This psalm was written by King David about his confidence in God. The verses that follow the one above are powerful, too: "No wonder my heart is glad, and I rejoice. My body rests in safety. For you will not leave my soul among the dead or allow your holy one to rot in the grave. You will show me the way of life, granting me the joy of your presence and the pleasures of living with you forever" (verses 9-11). King David had no doubt who God was!

Do you feel sure that God is who he says he is in scripture? Our doubt about God feeds our fears and anxieties. We question whether he is able to help us, or will provide for our needs. That insecurity creates confusion, which feeds fear and anxiety. When we can rest in the truth about who God is, there will be peace in our life. While this doesn't mean everything will go our way, it does mean that the foundation of our life is sure.

If you have unanswered questions about God, begin today by reading in scripture about who God is. Learn more about what he says in his Word. Share with friends who are believers and ask them about what they have experienced in their walk with the Lord. Your knowledge of God will grow as you continue in your relationship with him and his Word for as long as you live.

Let us occupy ourselves entirely in knowing God. The more we know Him, the more we will desire to know Him. As love increases with knowledge, the more we know God, the more we will truly love Him. We will learn to love Him equally in times of distress or in times of great joy.

Brother Lawrence

In making Himself known to us, He stays by the familiar pattern of personality. He communicates with us through the avenues of our minds, our wills, and our emotions.

A. W. Tozer

One of the most wonderful things about knowing God is that there's always so much more to know, so much more to discover. Just when we least expect it, He intrudes into our neat and tidy notions about who He is and how He works.

Joni Eareckson Tada

## For further reflection

Romans 12:1-2; Jeremiah 31:33-34; 1 John 1:6-7

## TODAY'S PRAYER

Heavenly Father, help me to know you more every day. Thank you for your love for me and for your faithfulness. Amen.

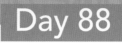

# Lord of Peace

*May the Lord of peace himself give you*
*his peace at all times and in every situation.*
*The Lord be with you all.*

2 THESSALONIANS 3:16

"Prince of Peace" is one of the names used to describe Jesus. In this passage, the apostle Paul refers to him as the Lord of peace. What a great description! Someone who can provide peace and is peace—that is Jesus.

This promise of peace is for you—at all times and in every situation. Do you need to hear that today? Is peace elusive for you? Anxiety can rob us of our peace, causing us to fret about things that are beyond our control. We can trust these things to the Lord of peace, because he is faithful.

If you are experiencing a storm in your life, Jesus is the peace in the midst of your storm. Are you fearing the unknown future? You can trust it to a known and powerful Lord. When we accept the peace of God, it is a gift to be opened every day—and sometimes each minute of the day! The challenge is for you to accept the gift of peace he is offering.

We are not at peace with others because we are not at peace with ourselves, and we are not at peace with ourselves because we are not at peace with God.

Thomas Merton

God's peace is not the calm after the storm. It's the steadfastness during it.

Michelle Bengston

Christ alone can bring lasting peace—peace with God—peace among men and nations—and peace within our hearts. He transcends the political and social boundaries of our world. God loves you and wants you to experience peace and life—abundant and eternal.

Billy Graham

## FOR FURTHER REFLECTION

Philippians 4:7; John 14:27; Romans 5:1-2

### TODAY'S PRAYER

Lord of Peace, I pray that I will experience your peace every day of my life. Help me to trust you in the storm, knowing you will make all things right. Amen.

# Get Moving

*"When we were at Mount Sinai, the Lord our God
said to us, 'You have stayed at this mountain long
enough. It is time to break camp and move on.'"*

<small>Deuteronomy 1:6-7a</small>

Stuck is a difficult place to be. We can get there through many different roads with names like fear, worry, loss, and control. What would your "road name" be? Sometimes the place we are stuck is comfortable, familiar, and "safe," which doesn't sound like a bad place at all. However, the place called stuck is exactly that; fixed, immovable, trapped.

It seems like you would want to stay in a place of comfort, right? That's what the Israelites thought after following Moses into the desert on their journey to the Promised Land. They were headed in the right direction, but at some point they got comfortable. God had something better in mind.

Have you gotten stuck in your anxieties, not sure of what direction to take in your life? You may have made yourself as comfortable as possible in order to settle down your fear, which sort of makes sense. Why would anyone want to feel anxious or afraid? The challenge is that you can get stuck in your life, depending on your own strength to journey through life. God has more for you, a place of freedom and purpose. He will lead you and provide direction for a life that is full and free! Will you get moving?

Not making a decision is actually a decision. It's the decision to stay the same.

Lysa TerKeurst

Just because God's path isn't always understandable doesn't mean it's not the right path.

Anonymous

If we wait until we're ready, we'll be waiting for the rest of our lives.

Lemony Snicket

## FOR FURTHER REFLECTION

Isaiah 30:21; Luke 1:78-79; John 12:24-26

### TODAY'S PRAYER

Lead me, Lord—I will follow. Help me to recognize where I am stuck and lead me to the place you have planned for me. Help me to live my life for your purpose and experience the freedom you died for me to have. I trust you with my life. Amen.

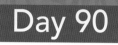

# Day 90

## Powerful

*Confess your sins to each other and pray for each
other so that you may be healed. The earnest
prayer of a righteous person has great
power and produces wonderful results.*

<small>JAMES 5:16</small>

The power of connection cannot be overstated.
Sometimes it is the most difficult healing path to
take. If there are people you talk with daily, you
may assume that you are in close relationships. However,
are those conversations with people in whom you trust
and confide? Do you pray together? Do they really know
what is in your heart and on your mind?

You need many different types of connections in your life.
There are the folks you see regularly—from the bus driver,
mail carrier, and barista to your neighbors, relatives, and
church family. Are there other people with whom you have
closer relationships, like a spouse or best friend? (Sometimes
those are the same person, but many times, unfortunately,
not.) When another person knows you fully and offers you
care and love without judgment, it is powerful! Perhaps you
provide that blessing in someone else's life. As we share our
lives together we experience peace and we feel heard and
cared for, which can ease our fear and anxiety.

In this world that celebrates individuality, some of us miss
out on the power of connecting with people in close,
life-long relationships. They take time, space, and energy
that you may be devoting to other aspects of your life. You

don't need to have a great number of close relationships—maybe two or three with people you trust who really know you. Begin today to cultivate the powerful gift we have of sharing life with other people!

Friendship is born at that moment when one man says to another, "What! You too? I thought that no one but myself . . ."

C. S. Lewis

A friend is someone who understands your past, believes in your future, and accepts you just the way you are.

Unknown

From my experience, loneliness isn't necessarily caused by a lack of people but is more an inner ache caused by a fractured soul. The question, Is this all there is? rumbles through the corridors of our minds.

Patsy Clairmont

## FOR FURTHER REFLECTION

Proverbs 17:17; 1 Thessalonians 5:11;
Colossians 3:12-14

### TODAY'S PRAYER

Lord, thank you for your friendship. Help me to connect with others, and to trust that you have created me for relationships. Help me to discern, trust, and share with people you have placed in my life. May these relationships bring you glory. Amen.

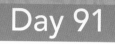

# Stability

*Jesus Christ is the same yesterday, today, and forever.*

Hebrews 13:8

One factor of anxiety and fear is the feeling of instability in your life. You may not be quite sure of yourself, not quite sure of your surroundings or your future or your ability to deal with various areas of your life. Life can feel as if there is a secret key that you can't find, or a trigonometry problem you cannot solve (unless, of course, math is your area of expertise!). If you could just figure out what is making you feel this way you would make the changes needed to feel better.

As you search for a resolution to your anxiety, you might need to try something for more than a day. You might need to go to the counselor for more than one visit. You might need to ask for more help than you feel comfortable doing. Here's the good news—Jesus, the Savior of your life, is the same always. He is the stable foundation for your life. You can build your life knowing that even when things feel uncertain, you're on solid ground.

When you are dealing with anxiety in your life, it can be helpful to identify the places in your life where you have stability. Your faith in Jesus isn't based on your perfection, it is the free gift of God for you. Continue to build your life on this truth, spending time in Bible study and prayer with friends who share your faith.

I had struggled so hard and so long that I had simply exhausted myself, only to find that God had all the time in the world to wait for me to allow Him to free me.

Michelle McKinney Hammond

Too often we want clarity and God wants us to come closer.

Ann Voskamp

I came to think of God as more of a gracious friend who was accompanying me on this journey, a friend who wanted to carry my burdens and speak into my life and shape me into who I really was and who I would become.

Joanna Gaines

## FOR FURTHER REFLECTION

Isaiah 26:3; Psalm 37:7; Jeremiah 17:7-8

## TODAY'S PRAYER

Thank you, Lord, for being my firm foundation upon which I can build my life. Help me and direct my way as I navigate through the issues I need to address. Thank you for your consistency and grace in my life. Amen.

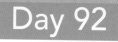

# Surefooted

*The Sovereign LORD is my strength! He makes me as surefooted as a deer, able to tread upon the heights.*

HABAKKUK 3:19

There is something that needs to be said about grace. Of course, the grace of God is an amazing gift to each of us, but the subject here is a different kind of grace—*gracefulness*, the ability to move about in the world without tripping up all the time. Anxious thoughts can create a feeling of clumsiness in how we move through life, and we second-guess everything we do or say. It causes us to doubt ourselves, our abilities, and our worth and value, so much so that we may second-guess everything we do or say.

God created you with gifts, talents, and love to share with others. We all have some doubts about who we are or how we go about the day. We need to fire the committee in our head that judges us on everything! No one is perfect; all of us need help in our lives. The highlight reels we see on social media are just that—the highlights. Everyone has struggles that they are not going to share with their audience. Recognize when you are harshly judging yourself, and be kind.

As you begin to receive the grace that God has for you, and recognize your worth, you will begin to experience peace. You will have a greater acceptance of yourself as well as others, knowing we are all on a path unique to us and learning along the way.

Grace is the voice that calls us to change and then gives us the power to pull it off.

Max Lucado

Grace releases and affirms. It doesn't smother. Grace values the dignity of individuals. It doesn't destroy. Grace supports and encourages. It isn't jealous or suspicious.

Chuck Swindoll

Through many dangers, toils and snares, I have already come; 'Tis grace has brought me safe thus far and grace will lead me home.

John Newton

## FOR FURTHER REFLECTION

2 Corinthians 12:9; Hebrews 4:16; Romans 5

### TODAY'S PRAYER

Thank you, Jesus, for the grace you give freely! Help me be strengthened in my awareness of your love and mercy for me, that I may live and move in your spirit. Amen.

# Identity

*"For in him we live and move and exist. As some of
your own poets have said, 'We are his offspring.'"*

ACTS 17:28

When you talk about yourself, what do you say? Do you describe your career roles, family roles, titles, perhaps a diagnosis? The way we talk about ourselves to others—and more importantly, in our own thoughts—has a powerful influence in our lives. Have you ever complimented someone only to have them reject it? Do you ever do that sort of thing? Are you unable to see what others are saying is to be celebrated in you? Being able to receive compliments is a skill some people never develop if the story in their own mind about themselves is negative.

The power of our identity affects us at a core level. If you identify primarily with your career—for instance, "I'm a banker"—it leaves out so much of who you really are. It tells us what you do, not necessarily who or what you love. When we know who we are—when we accept who we are *at this moment*—we are able to be aware of our current need. When we feel afraid, we can identify the fear, ask for help, and discern what we need in order to feel safe. There isn't anything 'masking' our true self. If we are doubtful of our value, we question our ability to make wise decisions. That, in turn, increases our anxiety.

Want to know your identity? You are first and foremost a child of the Most High God! He created you with gifts and talents, and loves you so much he gave his Son, Jesus, for your redemption. When you believe this to your core, you are receiving the truth about your identity. You will be able to have peace with yourself and others.

If your identity is found in Christ, then it matters less and less what people think of you.

Leonard Sweet

If you accept what people call you, you will start to believe it. Find your identity in Christ, not in what others say.

Joyce Meyer

The next time you stand in front of a mirror and want to scream, try to remember that God made that face. That smile. Those big eyes . . . and chubby cheeks. You are His creation, called to reflect Him. Spiritual transformation doesn't come from a diet program, a bottle, a makeover, or mask. It comes from an intimate relationship with the Savior. He . . . appreciates us for who we really are. So, we can too.

Luci Swindoll

## FOR FURTHER REFLECTION

2 Corinthians 5:17; Jeremiah 1:5; 1 John 3:1-3

### TODAY'S PRAYER

Thank you, Lord, for your grace and mercy! Help me know who I am in you, and to accept your love and forgiveness, in order to fulfill your call on my life. Amen.

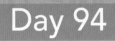
# Transparency

*Search me, O God, and know my heart; test me
and know my anxious thoughts. Point out
anything in me that offends you, and lead
me along the path of everlasting life.*

PSALM 139:23-24

Many times, when we feel anxiety and fear, we want to hide. We don't want to be seen in our state of worry, and we are hoping that we can muster the strength to get through the day, or the next hour. The truth is, in these moments we need to be seen and heard, to be able to know that we are cared for. God sees you and knows your needs.

Our anxious thoughts can cause us to get caught up in escaping, looking for ways to numb out: we may hide in alcohol, drugs, food, sex, shopping, and so on. This helps for the time being but not in the long run. What if you could find relief for your anxiety rather than numbing the feelings? A practice—a plan in your life that will help you with the anxiety—can provide peace.

The 12 steps that recovery programs use can offer a structure in which you can be seen and heard, even if you are not using drugs or alcohol to numb your pain. The recovery process helps you connect with the God who created you and knows your heart. In the verses above, the psalmist expresses an invitation for "God to search and know my heart." Would you be willing to ask God to search your heart? The goals are to find the path to life, to be able to connect with people who can share your journey, and to trust God in every part of your life.

There is nothing God doesn't know about your life. You may know the past and present, but God also knows the future. Choose today to walk securely—not in what you know, but in what you believe.

David Jeremiah

It's not about finding ways to avoid God's judgment and feeling like a failure if you don't do everything perfectly. It's about fully experiencing God's love and letting it perfect you. It's not about being somebody you are not. It's about becoming who you really are.

Stormie Omartian

Sociologists have a theory of the looking-glass self: you become what the most important person in your life (wife, father, boss, etc.) thinks you are. How would my life change if I truly believed the Bible's astounding words about God's love for me, if I looked in the mirror and saw what God sees?

Philip Yancey

### FOR FURTHER REFLECTION

John 3:16; Zephaniah 3:17; Nehemiah 9:19-20

## TODAY'S PRAYER

Lord, I open my heart to you, trusting your grace and mercy. You know me completely. Help me as I heal and grow. Lead me in your way, for your glory. Amen.

# Joy

*His anger lasts only a moment, but his favor
lasts a lifetime! Weeping may last through
the night, but joy comes with the morning.*

PSALM 30:5

There are some hardships in life that it feels as though we will never get over. If you told someone stories about what you have lived through, they would totally understand. Anxiety and fear start to fill in the spaces that difficulties create, and you might think this is what your life will always be like from now on. Whether you feel guilty because of a bad choice, or hurt because of what happened to you, there is hope.

God is not surprised by your life—nothing has caught him off duty. This is comforting and frustrating all at the same time. If God knew what you experienced, why didn't he stop it? Where was God when you were going through the worst days of your life? God was there, hurting for you, holding you, and providing a way out. Your fears and worries were not forgotten by God. Eventually you begin to heal, and life looks and feels different than before.

If you are feeling like nothing can ever remove the pain and hurt you have gone through, please reconsider. Your anxious thoughts, your fear, and your pain can all be turned to joy as God works through the healing. There are many accounts in the Bible about devastation and redemption. Jesus' death on the cross is the ultimate healing story! God is still working, and if you will allow him to heal your hurts, you will experience joy once again.

I choose joy . . . I will invite my God to be the God of circumstance. I will refuse the temptation to be cynical . . . the tool of the lazy thinker. I will refuse to see people as anything less than human beings, created by God. I will refuse to see any problem as anything less than an opportunity to see God.

Max Lucado

Live for today but hold your hands open to tomorrow. Anticipate the future and its changes with joy. There is a seed of God's love in every event, every circumstance, every unpleasant situation in which you may find yourself.

Barbara Johnson

When we are powerless to do a thing, it is a great joy that we can come and step inside the ability of Jesus.

Corrie ten Boom

## FOR FURTHER REFLECTION

Psalm 143:8; Psalm 23; Isaiah 54:10

### TODAY'S PRAYER

Heavenly Father, I praise you for the joy that you give. Help me find your joy in the difficult days and in days of doubt. You sustain me with your love, and for this I am grateful. Amen.

# Mercy

*That is why the LORD says, "Turn to me now, while there is time. . . . Don't tear your clothing in your grief, but tear your hearts instead." Return to the LORD your God, for he is merciful and compassionate, slow to get angry and filled with unfailing love. He is eager to relent and not punish.*

JOEL 2:12–13

To know God and how he thinks about us is a powerful healing force in our lives. Knowing the depths of his love for us and understanding the grace he offers and the joy we bring to him changes our perspective on life. However, if you have the wrong view of God it can create distance, insecurity, and fear in your life.

Do you experience the presence of God as peaceful or condemning? Where did you learn about God, and have you explored the Bible to find out who he is? It is crucial to be able to trust God with the trials we are going through. Knowing that the Almighty God loves us and cares for us gives us peace and strength for the journey. It is his great mercy that allows us to have a relationship with our Holy God. What an amazing truth!

When anxiety and fear fill your heart, return to the One who can provide comfort for your soul. The Creator God has you in the palm of his hand and will provide mercy and compassion for your needs, today and every day of your life.

But here's the thing: pretty good people do not need Jesus. He came for the lost. He came for the broken. In his love for us he came to usher us into his foundness and wholeness.

Tish Harrison Warren

From God's perspective, one hidden act of repentance, one little gesture of selfless love, one moment of true forgiveness is all that is needed to bring God from his throne to run to his returning son and to fill the heavens with sounds of divine joy.

Henri J. M. Nouwen

God will not force himself upon anyone. It is our part to believe; it is our part to receive. No one can do it for us.

Billy Graham

## For further reflection

1 Peter 5:6-10; Psalm 46:10; Hebrews 10:22-23

### TODAY'S PRAYER

Heavenly Father, thank you for your love for me. Help me as I seek you to find you. I praise your name forever. Amen.

# Faith

*Faith shows the reality of what we hope for;*
*it is the evidence of things we cannot see.*

HEBREWS 11:1

Unbelief is the opposite of faith. Unbelief may also reflect a lack of confidence. You might associate unbelief with mistrust—not believing things are as they seem, or just not trusting at all. When you are a person of faith, and you sometimes struggle with unbelief, does it mean you are sinning? Are you never supposed to doubt?

In chapter 11 of Hebrews, which is known as the "Hall of Faith," we read accounts of people who trusted God with their lives even though they did not know how things would turn out. Verse 6 reads: "And it is impossible to please God without faith. Anyone who wants to come to him must believe that God exists and that he rewards those who sincerely seek him." It is impossible to please God without faith?—what? When we read about these people, we know the end of their stories—but they didn't. During the time they were following God, they likely experienced anxiety and fear, but they followed God anyway.

That's the point. Do it afraid. Even when you know God and trust his will for your life, you will have times of doubt. Just don't stay there. Know that even when events do not make sense to you in the moment, God has a bigger plan in mind. Trust him every step of the way and watch your faith and belief in God grow! You will become more confident because you know your faith is sure.

Can I trust God? Trust is an essential ingredient to surrender. You won't surrender to God unless you trust him, but you can't trust him until you know him better. Fear keeps us from surrendering, but love casts out all fear. The more you realize how much God loves you, the easier surrender becomes.

Rick Warren

If you are faced with the question of whether or not to surrender, make a determination to go on through the crisis, surrendering all that you have and all that you are to Him. And God will then equip you to do all that He requires of you.

Oswald Chambers

God has promised that whatever you face, you are not alone. He knows your pain. He loves you. And He will bring you through the fire.

Sheila Walsh

## FOR FURTHER REFLECTION

Ecclesiastes 3:1-14; Romans 12:2

### TODAY'S PRAYER

Lord, help my unbelief. I want to follow your will for my life. Help me to trust you more. I surrender my will and have decided to follow you all the days of my life. Amen.

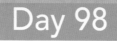

# Redemption

*I called on your name, LORD, from deep within the pit.*
*You heard me when I cried, "Listen to my pleading!*
*Hear my cry for help!" Yes, you came when I called;*
*you told me, "Do not fear." Lord, you have come to*
*my defense; you have redeemed my life.*

LAMENTATIONS 3:55-58

When we walk through a long season of fear and anxiety, we wonder if it is ever going to end. Maybe you have prayed and sought answers from books, people, and God, but still felt like no one would ever come to save you. When answers come, there is sweet relief. But while you are waiting for answers, your heartache and exhaustion are very real.

This passage is a promise that God hears you. He says, "do not fear." If you are still waiting for answers, it doesn't mean he hasn't heard you. Trust that God is coming to your defense, to save you and redeem your situation. If you are finding it hard to trust that God is working on your behalf, surrendering to him in the middle of the waiting can reduce your fear and anxiety. Just because you can't see God working doesn't mean that he is unaware of your need.

If this is where you are today, trust God to work in your life. One way to build your trust is to connect with people who can be your support. When we are in a pit, we can isolate ourselves and allow our whole life to be consumed with the problem we are praying about. You can decide today to make a move towards trusting God, knowing you cannot control it all, and that he hears your cry for help.

God doesn't stop the bad things from happening; that's never been part of the promise. The promise is: I am with you. I am with you now until the end of time.

Madeleine L'Engle

Live every day to fulfill your personal mission. God has a reason for whatever season you are living through right now. A season of loss or blessing? A season of activity or hibernation? A season of growth or incubation? You may think you're on a detour, but God knows the best way for you to reach your destination.

Barbara Johnson

To trust God in the light is nothing, but to trust Him in the dark—that is faith.

Charles Spurgeon

## FOR FURTHER REFLECTION

Psalm 28:7; Isaiah 41:10; John 14:1

### TODAY'S PRAYER

Lord God, I am crying out to you in my pain and distress. You know my situation and my fears. I release them to you knowing you will redeem this for your glory. Amen.

# Day 99

## Anticipation

*Hope deferred makes the heart sick,*
*but a dream fulfilled is a tree of life.*

PROVERBS 13:12

B ack in the 1970s, a ketchup commercial used Carly Simon's song "Anticipation" as the background music. She sang, "Anticipation is making me wait, keeping me waiting." We all know what it's like to wait for ketchup to finally come out of the bottle, so the song fit perfectly! Would that song be a good fit for the hopes and plans you have for your life? Waiting and wondering how things will turn out can create all kinds of anxiety.

This proverb states that waiting will make your heart sick. When you are hoping that something will turn out well, at the same time you may be feeling fearful that it won't go the way you expect. You may be anxiously awaiting the outcome of something big in your life. This literally can make you sick. You can get so focused on what may or may not happen that you are always distracted with worry.

Not everything we hope for will come to pass. We will learn how to accept that and move on in our lives. Other blessings will take place that we weren't looking for, as well as a few dreams that do come true. It is all part of life. Learning to accept that will help you manage your anxious heart. God is working all things for your good. Look forward to good things and recognize God's presence while you wait.

God doesn't grow tired of hearing our petitions. We are the ones that grow tired of petitioning. Keep praying. God hasn't stopped listening.

Jackie Hill Perry

Those times we find ourselves having to wait on others may be the perfect opportunities to train ourselves to wait on the Lord.

Joni Eareckson Tada

Waiting on God requires the willingness to bear uncertainty, to carry within oneself the unanswered question, lifting the heart to God about it whenever it intrudes upon one's thoughts.

Elisabeth Elliot

## For further reflection

Psalm 130:5-6; James 5:7-8; Romans 5:3-4

### TODAY'S PRAYER

Lord Jesus, I pray for patience in my time of waiting. I don't want to lose hope, which comes from trusting you. Help me to trust that you will work all things out for my good and for your glory. Amen.

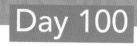

## Come Closer

*Come close to God, and God will come close to you.*

JAMES 4:8A

The truth is that God is an ever-present help in our time of need. However, our day-to-day reality is that many times we feel disconnected from God. In our anxiety and fear we don't "feel" the nearness of the One who loves and cares for us the most. We also tend to push away loved ones who want to offer consolation and support. This struggle—needing help, yet not seeking or accepting it—will keep us stuck.

How do you come close to God? When do you experience the presence of the Almighty? For some it is in nature. Others may feel closest to God in a church, while listening to music, or in some other personal way. There isn't a "right" way. But a close, personal relationship with the Most High God is something every one of us needs in our lives. Think about the last time you sensed the presence of God—where were you, what were you doing, and how did you experience God?

Today, come closer to the Lord. He is waiting wherever you are, and will be a constant source of strength. God loves you, has a plan for your life, and will never leave you nor forsake you. He will provide comfort and assurance in your life.

Sometimes God calms the storm, but sometimes God lets the storm rage and calms the frightened child.

Leslie Gould

Always, everywhere God is present, and always He seeks to discover Himself to each one.

A. W. Tozer

We need to find God, and he cannot be found in noise and restlessness. God is the friend of silence. See how nature—trees, flowers, grass—grows in silence; see the stars, the moon and the sun, how they move in silence. . . . We need silence to be able to touch souls.

Mother Teresa

## FOR FURTHER REFLECTION

Psalm 23; Philippians 4:6-7; Matthew 11:28-30

### TODAY'S PRAYER

Thank you, Lord, for your presence. As I seek you may I find comfort, strength, and wisdom as you have promised. Thank you for all you have done for me. May I bring you glory in my life. Amen.

# DEVOTIONALS FROM
## STEPHEN ARTERBURN

### *100 Days of Character* Daily Devotional

Imitation Leather, 208 pages, 5" x 8"

**ISBN: 9781628624953**

### *100 Days of Prayer* Daily Devotional

Imitation Leather, 208 pages, 5" x 8"

**ISBN: 9781628624281**

### *100 Days of Peace* Daily Devotional

Imitation Leather, 208 pages, 5" x 8"

**ISBN: 9781628624960**

### *100 Days of Healing* Daily Devotional

Imitation Leather, 208 pages, 5" x 8"

**ISBN: 9781628624946**

www.hendricksonrose.com